AFTER THE RAIN FALLS

Timothy Moore

Copyright © 2024 by Timothy Moore
Foreword Copyright © 2024 by Dr. Ernest L. Gibson III
Epilogue Copyright © 2024 by Dr. Rashawn Ray

All rights reserved. No part of this book may be used or reproduced in any manner whatsoever without the written permission of the author and/or publisher

Victory Publishing Co
PO Box 25722
Memphis, TN 38125
www.victorypublishingco.com

Edited by Amber Carter with ANC Proofreading Services

ISBN (paberback): 9781736603093
ISBN (ebook): 9781964284002

Printed in the United States of America

Dedication

To my daughters, my love, and everyone that has ever chased a dream.
May joy find you in this life.

Table of Contents

Dedication 3

Preface 9

Foreword 11

Chapter One: Acknowledge The Storm 15

    Struggle 16

    Make Believe 17

    Wild Things 20

    Treasure 24

    Seizures 25

    Ashes 28

    Worthy 30

    Cancer 33

    Still Born 35

Chapter Two: Awareness Within the Chaos 37

    Big Boy Blues 38

    Sticks And Stones 40

    The Villain 44

    When The Pandemic Came 45

    Stardust 48

    Absent Notes 50

    She 52

    For The Black Girls That Never Come Home 53

Black Girl Magic 57

Graffiti and Teddy Bears 58

Twenty-Three 60

My First Love Letter 63

Invisible Hoodies 66

Black Diamonds 69

Before We Grew Up 70

Dear Son 73

Birthday Candles 76

Chapter Three: The Awakening - After The Rain Falls 79

#Issasnack 80

Just Beautiful 83

Secrets 86

I Loved Once 87

#Metoo 91

Chameleon 95

Dear Black Men: That's Gay 98

Phobias 103

Tears For My Daughter 107

Three Letters 110

Scars 114

A Love Letter To America 116

Smiles 119

Enter 120

Spades 123

Stained Glass 126

Cry 129

    For My Grandpa..133
    Wrong Woman..137
    When They Tell You That You Are Dying................................. 138
    To My Father 141

Epilogue...145

Acknowledgements 149

Preface

For every reader who has questioned, "What do men feel?" I offer this collection of poems, essays and ideas. I am not every man but a lot of these circumstances, ideas, and life moments exist in and around my brothers. My goal was to shine a light on topics that we as a society dim or intentionally hold in the dark. This collection represents my journey through this life. It is a love letter to masculinity, family and all the beautiful women that have poured into my life. It is a sincere hallelujah of resurrection from my broken.

To my parents who never stopped believing in me- Thank you. They say printed words last forever. I want the world to know that I owe you both so much for every award that ever came my way. You all were the inspiration for my success.

Love and light to my siblings, my precious love Andrea, my god-parents (The Jones family), Christopher "Truth B. Told" Owens, the Hall family, my fraternity line brothers, and my daughters: Iyanla, Asha and Imani. You all have been my village.

TIMOTHY "URBAN THOUGHTS" MOORE

To my brothers of Alpha Phi Alpha Fraternity, Inc., There are so many men, mentors and so many souls that have impacted me to be a man that continually seeks to transcend. It is in that pursuit that I have found happiness to become more than what I was or am. I praise God for thee.

To my beautiful three daughters- I pray when God and this Universe calls me home after a long life that this work captures who I was. More than that, I wish that the words show you all how much I loved you and how the three of you inspired me to be a better man than I ever thought possible.

Honestly, I don't have many more words so this may be the shortest preface in the history of books. All the words I hold for now are in this book. It is my soul bared raw and unapologetic between the pages. Black beings held in space. They are waiting to find a home in your heart for you to consider.

Within this book, I pray that the words hold you. May the words encourage you as they have me through the storms. I pray that more words come for my next journey. For now, I simply say thank-you for allowing me space in your life. I thank the Creator God for all that has blessed me with this ability. This book is for after the rain falls. May joy find you in this life and beyond every storm that comes your way.

Best Regards,
Timothy "Urban Thoughts" Moore

#Onward

Foreword

Reading for the Wanderer

I like to imagine that poems are like wanderers. That they are forever searching until they find a place they can call home. In a sense, poems are born before poets, they usher in a new way of artistic being, they call forth their subjects. *After the Rain Falls* is evidence of this. It is a collection of poems that reveals the reality of how language often chooses its vessels, how the art of conjuring is always already pre-ordained by the words' search for someone to help them mean. Timothy Moore is lucky in this way. For the words that are to follow have chosen him, have deemed him worthy to offer them to this world and its readers, have found in him the artist who will help them to mean something more, perhaps for someone else. We, of course, are luckier. As readers of these amazing poems, we have the privilege of invitation. Moore herein has bore both his strength and vulnerability, has dared to peel back the cloaks of comfort that keeps most men silent, and has, indeed, invited us into a sacred space. Within these pages, Moore constructs an altar of language, and in a tone at times as faint as the voice of dawn, he asks for us to partake. And so, whether ready or hungry, we shall.

TIMOTHY "URBAN THOUGHTS" MOORE

Beyond the Performance, Beneath the Text
I remember the first time I met Timothy – it was through the sound of his voice. Sure, I heard the emcee announce him as "Urban Thoughts," and I was curious to see what this poet had to offer to the crowd that night in Memphis, Tennessee. However, I did not fully see him until I felt him, until his voice announced him as an artist, until his words took hold of my attention. I sat in the dimly lit space, and after listening to a round of poets, I did not expect to hear his poetic vocality. His utterance had a very particular texture, almost as if his spoken words were tactile, like if you were close enough you could literally feel them upon your skin. This way of touching, of moving the listener from stranger to witness, of beckoning the curious into an intimate space of sharing is the wonder of Timothy "Urban Thoughts" Moore. And while he possessed those signature traits of dope spoken word artists, those elements that ensure high scores from slightly intoxicated judges, there was also something more. There is always something more with him. I imagine the words demand it. And again, we are lucky.

Performance and printed poetry are very different genres. Rare is the poet skilled enough to deliver in both mediums. The rhythm demanded by spoken word artistry – the way it calls on the body for its form and its movement, the leaning into the performative – often runs counter to the specificity of craft in the written form – the quiet reliance and trust that must be placed within the reader, the vulnerability of the body's absence in the text's most naked state. When the adornments of orality are stripped from a poetic piece, the printed poem must offer something beneath its text, must whisper to its reader to dig for something beyond its surface. This is not easy, especially for those artists whose meaning is amplified by affective tonality and voice. Yet, despite such complexities, Moore has offered his readers a reason to sit and delve, a reason to listen to his quiet.

Journeying for Joy

In the dedication to this collection, Moore writes, "May joy find you in this life." Similar to those poems in search for the artist that will help them into meaning, joy is also searching. More than anything else, *After the Rain Falls* captures a Black man's journeying for joy. Moore does not promise it, does not offer you rainbows without storms, does not skip to the silver linings. Instead, he takes us on his pursuit to discover what the other side of heartache looks like, to see what light might come after moments of darkness, to feel how softly God can hold you after life hits you hard. Taking the reader along a narrative arc that moves through acknowledgement, awareness and awakening, Moore scripts the human compulsion to question, to mourn, to love, to break, and to breathe once more. This collection captures the complexity of loss, as it fights to find the language of eulogy, of mourning, of how to find a life after. It textualizes Black male vulnerability, showcasing how wounds often form from a disavowal of tenderness, how tethered we are to sexism and homophobia. It makes real the ugliness of life, stretches pain across betrayal, and meanders through a series of aches. And yet, it still finds its way back from the depths, as it gestures for and grinds to the possibilities and potencies of joy. In the end, Moore insists for us to journey.

TIMOTHY "URBAN THOUGHTS" MOORE

I like to imagine that poems are like wanderers. I sense they are forever searching for the right person to shape into an artist. I also imagine that what poems look for is the right hand. They must find someone whose hand is both strong and gentle, rough and soft, someone who has experienced the world in a way to promise you that life is worth fight for and fighting back to, so to speak. Timothy's hands are purposed for poetic pursuit, are destined to touch the minds and hearts of his readers. I remember the first time we both surrendered to friendship, the first time we truly hugged. I remembered thinking, this is a man beautiful enough to hug the world. And I was right. *After the Rain Falls* will undoubtedly break you open. But, if you walk with Moore from the pain in the beginning to the culminating love in the end, his words will not only hold you, they will also hug you back. They will hug you back whole.

-Dr. Ernest L. Gibson III

Dr. Ernest L. Gibson III received his PhD in Afro-American studies from the University of Massachusetts – Amherst. He is the author of *Salvific Manhood: James Baldwin's Novelization of Male Intimacy* (University of Nebraska Press, 2019), and has published on James Baldwin, W.E.B. Du Bois, and *Scandal*. An interdisciplinary scholar by training, his research lies at the intersections of literary, cultural, and queer theories, and often pivots on questions of manhood, masculinity, and vulnerability. He is currently at work on his second book project, tentatively entitled, *Dark Penmanship: Afro-Ontology, Resistance, and Freedom* (Biography via Auburn University directory). He is a profound thinker, scholar, and poet who is sought after for his research on masculinity and vulnerability.

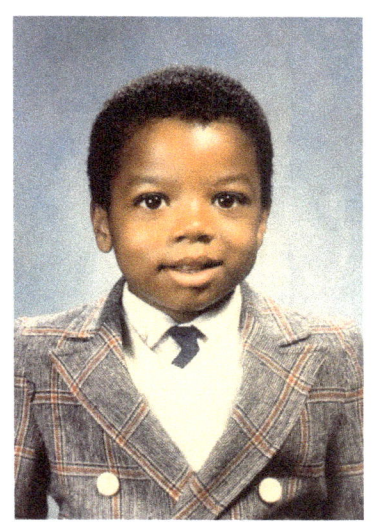

Chapter One:
Acknowledge The Storm

Sometimes, pain just is.
There is no refuge.
Just a deep internal acknowledgement-
That this can't be all there is.

Struggle

I envy the grain of salt that enters the oyster's mouth
that becomes a pearl.

I envy the lump of black coal that is buried under earth
that becomes a diamond.

I envy the caterpillar that dies in the cocoon
that becomes a butterfly.

At least they know deep down
that they will survive the tribulations and trials,
to be made beautiful.

Make Believe

My favorite moments of childhood were playing make believe.
Pretending to be Spiderman,
Hanging off furniture that became sides of skyscrapers,
My mother yelling, "Boy- If you don't get yo' butt off of my couch!"
Me – jumping, landing, posing, "Yes- Ma'am."

Even had the full costume,
With the Nerf gun web shooters.
Depending on the storyline,
With the flick of a wrist,
My brothers became either:
Bank robbers to punish or people to save.
I became really good at playing make believe.
In fact, as an adult,
I still do.

When people ask: How are you feeling?"
Most expect you to say, "I'm okay,"
Even if you aren't.
In the South, answering honestly leads to awkward conversations
About praying the sadness away
Like these knees and palms ain't got callouses
from pressing these frustrations in between Asé and Amens.

TIMOTHY "URBAN THOUGHTS" MOORE

I've taught myself to be quiet than to voice
That I am one of the 300 million diagnosed with depression.
Even still- it's difficult for me to give it name,
Or space,
Or to admit that sometimes, these tears just come
Like long lost friends that ain't good for nothing
But reminding you of the past fun that you used to have,
Or worse moments that you don't even realize that there
Are tears on your cheeks,
Or sadness that has no origin.
It just is,
A black hole hovering over a black body,
Daring any and all not to come to close less they be consumed.

In moments of depression,
I forget that I can breathe.
Suffocating seems so normal.
My lungs lose muscle memory of how to inflate.
My chest becomes a casket for my breath to bury itself in.
Saying "I'm awesome" is me pushing back the walls
That are always closing in.
Even when I count to ten like my therapist said,
Alright is easier than stomaching that over 800,000 Americans
Struggle to be "alright"
And that nearly one person every forty seconds
Decides to disappear into total eclipse.

I embraced the moons shadow once.
Slit my wrist 'til the blood painted a crescent on my hand.
I empathize with Atlas.

AFTER THE RAIN FALLS

I know how the weight of the world feels.
On those days "good" is just
Getting out of a bed that on most mornings seems
To be more quicksand than comfort.

"Good" are the days I just get to teach in my classroom
"Good" are the moments, I get to ask kids:
"How are you?"
Days that I get to paint a smile on my face
that is often more times Joker than honest laughter.

In my classroom,
I get to silence my fears and become someone's hero.
I get to show them that no matter how bad life hurts
That you can get up one more time.
You can get up one more time.
You can get up.
And one day they will ask, "How are you?"
I'll stand shoulders back and say "I'm doing just fine,"
And mean it.

TIMOTHY "URBAN THOUGHTS" MOORE

Wild Things

(On June 12, 1999 -my best friend Willie Brown, Jr., left a suicide note with the quote:
"I have never seen a wild thing feel sorry for itself.")

I have never seen a wild thing feel sorry for itself,
Shed tears for itself,
Or worry about its health,
And I've been a wild thing all my life.
And all my life, all I known was strife:
Heartbreak and tears.

My whole life, I've been battling this WILD THING
Like a game of chess
But it seems like all I've had was this dusty old bag of checkers to compete with, Maybe I was born the bastard son of Milton Bradley
Or the forgotten cousin of Nintendo,
Playing games with missing pieces -
Monopoly with no cash,
Shooting pool with curved sticks,
Matching shots of basketball with broken wrists,
nothing but bricks.

AFTER THE RAIN FALLS

Since birth, suicide claws gripping my umbilical cord,
A noose trying to hang me inside my mother's womb.
Since day one I was born cold,
Grandma praying on calloused knees
to Jesus hanging on walls- I breathed.

I know God is real cause I done seen Heaven and I've seen Hell.
Hell dwells -within the mirrored reflections of my smile.
See, I'm that wild thing dancing on razor blades.
The strange fruit from strange deferred dreams.
Blood on my leaves and blood on my root

Since the age of thirteen
I've filled enough prescriptions to build
a Wal-Mart pharmacy in powdered tears.
Y'all, truth is, sometimes I dream of being an angel
With a gas can in my right hand,
Lit matches in the left hand,
And I'm trying not to clap.
Not afraid to die, just afraid of not making it back into heaven.

I'm broken. Scarred arms.
Hidden stains of pill residue vomited back into t-shirts.
Washed empty bottles and shattered dreams stuffed into trash cans.
Pushed round back behind the grins.

TIMOTHY "URBAN THOUGHTS" MOORE

II.

I open the door. My baby girl hugs me.
She separates the decision of the gun in the closet
Or the knife in the drawer when she is not around.

Question: Have you ever been so close to death that you wanted it?
Ever contemplate suicide,
a piece of peace permanently between doing poetry pieces?
I have.

I've sat in the back seat of my truck and threw a brick at the gas pedal.
The only thing stopping me from dying was God
tipping my truck over from the weight of a daughter's prayers
to hear her father read her favorite book again.

Have you ever sat with a Wild Thing that no longer resides
In the pages of a book but the reflection of a look in a mirror,
From a shadow of a person you remember being happy some time ago?

My daughter speaks, breaking my thoughts
She stares at me.
Wild eyed, wondering why I hug her so tight when she visits.
Telling me to read to her: *Where the Wild Things Are.*

AFTER THE RAIN FALLS

I tell her, "Not today, Asha."
Today, I will read to you a poem about where the Wild Thing was
And how a daughter's hugs kept the monsters away from coming back home.

TIMOTHY "URBAN THOUGHTS" MOORE

Treasure

I buried my smile behind broken.
Forgot to mark an X,
Of where my happiness was.
Forgot what a smile is.

I've learned over years how to pretend well,
Look great even when sick or dying,
Or trying to be okay.
I buried my smile a while ago- somewhere.

AFTER THE RAIN FALLS

Seizures

The ground stops.
We stand in the aftermath.
We all now realize how it feels when your whole world shakes.
Sound crumbles into ash.

When the earthquake started,
No one really understood.
We all just stared,
As young folks do
when something new comes into community.

Memphis lives on fault lines.
We all knew deep down
That this day would come.

Almost like Angels collecting old debts
For killing a King's kid.
We knew when we made Martin martyr.
We watched blood fill foundations of racist.
Pyramids reformed to make skyscrapers with nice views.

Disturbances of lynched forgotten bones moved
for gentrification of neighborhoods to look better.

TIMOTHY "URBAN THOUGHTS" MOORE

When you remove the auction block dust,
Confederate symbols in parks lent their names to greenspaces
and when frustrated with the protests-just redline it all.

The old folks said it was God.
The scientist just nature.
That old priestess that plays with bones and herbs
said it was Mother Earth angry at all the drilling.

I believed all and none.
I believe it was you.
Screaming out that you are still here.
Violent protest of a body that betrays your voice.

Your vocal chords never adjusted to the faults of vibration.
Seismic collapses occur when the brain rattles too much.
You don't have the choice of the beauty of choosing silence.
You- stand mute,
Watching the ground make noise.
Isn't that the irony that everything is a symphony of sound around you.
Crashing it all down with each rumble.

Yet, you, friend stand still.
The Earth moving is familiar to you.
You do not fear what you know.
While we run and hide
And scream.

You, silent.

AFTER THE RAIN FALLS

You, calm.
Planted firm, you point a finger at your wheel chair.

The ground stops.
We stand in the aftermath.
We all now know how it feels-
When your whole world shakes.

TIMOTHY "URBAN THOUGHTS" MOORE

Ashes

There is still magic in your smoke.
Black girl magic transcending from pits.
Funny, how men try to contain fire
Like the sun name is not woman.

As if the moon, does not reflect the flame.
We control nothing.
Yet, we try. We place flame in metal boxes
Or cylinders on sticks.
Barbecuing flesh for us to consume.

How interesting for men to try to control flame.
How we manipulate temperatures
Until she burns out of control, raging,
Destroying all that try to warm by her side
Or get too close to her beauty
Or find themselves in love with the heat of her.
Cold calculating whimpers
Whipped into loud vengeance for the next.

Inferno erupting of volcanic ashes
Or love, or lust, or hate, or love
Or anything else that consumes.
There is magic behind the smoke
But it is so difficult to see,
Or feel behind the screen,

AFTER THE RAIN FALLS

Or to know what's real,
If all you can touch are the ashes.

TIMOTHY "URBAN THOUGHTS" MOORE

Worthy
(For my Grandpa Robert)

The doctors say, "Your heart will fail."
I think that your heart is just tired,
which is to say that you worked it so hard for over 80 years.
Each day giving a little more of it to people who were:
in need,
in your family,
in your eyesight,
Who were:
unworthy,
ungrateful,
or unfamiliar.

Yet, you still gave,
ironic, now when you need your heart back.
The doctors say you are too old:
to deserve,
to need,
or to be offered one,
which you understood.
Stoic and full of love, You said,
"Yeah, give it to the young ones,"
Which is to say- I have lived a blessed life.
Which is probably what Jesus said
When He sacrificed for us on a cross,
On a mountain that he didn't belong on.

AFTER THE RAIN FALLS

Ain't that just like a Black Man
to always provide what you want
and didn't know that you needed
from just a hard work ethic
giving all heart
and all the love
all the time?
Ain't that Christ like?

These mountains always come on the horizon.
They block our views sometimes
until you climb them and look back.
You see then- how beautiful the view is.
You see how far you have gone.
Others will see your path,
Dug in love.
Too stubborn to quit,
you keep fighting.
Your heart still has a little work to do
but while it beats let this poem be a balm.
Let it be a reminder of how your heart has inspired
us to do more with the hearts that beat for yours.

TIMOTHY "URBAN THOUGHTS" MOORE

A Haiku or a poem about life whichever you can figure out first

Time's fragile, our hands,
small. Body becomes wasting clay.
One chance. Be love, now.

AFTER THE RAIN FALLS

Cancer

(For Aunt Rose)

two seconds pass by slowly
gracefully touching one another
each just a millisecond from becoming lonely
lifetimes separated from the other
time mimics humans this way
dying without notice or at least warning
forsaking the heat of the sun
for the coolness of the night's embrace

one second fading threatening to leave
without the simplest of footprint or trace

we are all just remnants of one another she says
I guess that's why I feel her pain
there are 800 miles of space between Memphis and Alabama's
Cancer Unit

one millisecond defiantly challenging
death, doctors and time

TIMOTHY "URBAN THOUGHTS" MOORE

dreams and prayers hold my fears now
I see you there etched inside my teardrops
you are laying there
in your courage
while I sit here, sleeping

in my dreams
I am still by your bedside
still praying
refusing to think of losing you

when I wake
I will hear the quiet
and miss you

AFTER THE RAIN FALLS

Still Born
(for my son Emmanuel)

There is a diligent patience and knowing about the turtle
Aware of all, full of love,
of good fortune and purpose.
Walking carefully through life
and sorrow and joy,
Protected by shell or self or God.
Bound to a home, he will always know.
I am jealous.

I am not turtle.
Never really knew home or love or God.
Too much man wanting to make right.
Make change or a difference.
Between grief & sorrow,
There is a lesson that the turtle
Didn't tell me of when we met in the woods.

In its community,
Turtle refused to acknowledge me.
Ignored man.
Didn't tell me how to find home or purpose
And I asked about God and love.

He grew angry at my impatience
To stumble in the woods.
I run too much trying to push through this life and trees.

TIMOTHY "URBAN THOUGHTS" MOORE

I haven't found peace here.
Where we all are.
You, who never breathed,
Never knew turtle.
Never found home.
You only met God, again.
Never met me.
If this is God's work to make all connected between breaths
Then I question did she clock out too early to get to the weekend?
I imagine that the turtle knows
Or at least has known about the sorrow of burying
sons born too cold to swim in this world.
I asked the turtle to teach me love.
Asked about patience,
Instead turtle taught me a lesson
About forgiveness of self,
Of God
Then I talked to God
Or nature
If turtles be God
Or if I be made in his image
Then why could I only create
And not sustain you beyond a moment
To know God
Or turtles
Or father
Or your name
Or where home is

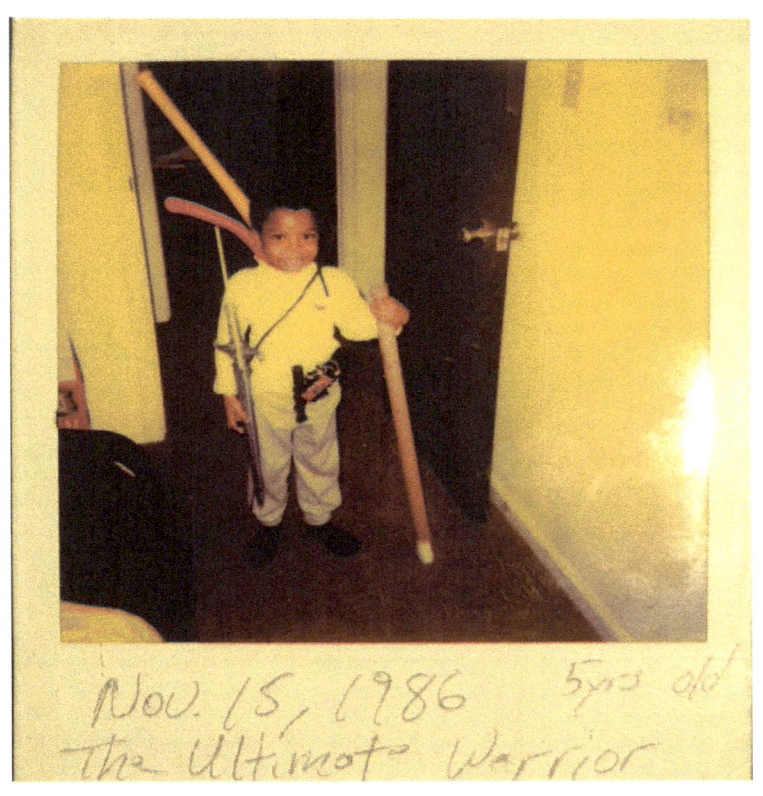

Chapter Two:

Awareness Within the Chaos

At the eye of a hurricane is peace.
Outside of that peace is chaos.
We owe it to ourselves to create our own safe space.
Even when the storm is raging outside of us:
We deserve love in the midst of.

Big Boy Blues

Sometimes people ask about my walk or make fun of my weight. Ninety-nine percent of the time- I don't care. BUT today someone who battles anxiety, depression, and life couldn't ignore the statements and laughter. The statements made me want to bark back the list of things I've survived or what I'm going through now. Hurt worse cause I expected better from them. A lot like how I expect my own black people not to call me the N-Word with the -er or the -a ending. I don't like that word as much as I dislike the truth that I am fat.

It is always uncouth or wrong to call a woman BIG. People make fun of the waddle that occurs on my bad days. It is a slow shift of my weight if I have to stand for long periods of time. My legs grow tired from a spinal cord attached to nerves that fire off too quickly. We quickly call men big dog, big fella, and other names without ever knowing their struggle behind the BIG. As if we (the big men) don't have egos, struggles or days where we get mad at certain shirts not fitting.

Even now I've lost 120 pounds and all I can fixate on tonight is how this fibromyalgia and the nodules in my neck that have to be surgically removed are destroying my body. I don't have much. I give more away then I keep. I find myself too busy working on community to worry about self. I have finally arrived to the conclusion that it is okay to worry about myself. It is okay to be tired.

AFTER THE RAIN FALLS

Funny-how we can watch Avengers and never clearly see the message. We can scream Wakanda forever but never love Black folks. We pronounce that we should heal our Black men but never ask what do you need to heal? Instead, we create the cycle of anger and broken emotions that keep us triggered. We hold back from transcending into our best forms. One day, I wonder if it will be all worth it? Or when I die- will they just say-we need a double wide casket cause his dreams were equally as big as him. Yeah, I'm tired and most days, I say nothing but today hurts. Writing is my healing. My therapy is being honest on social media, in poems and now this book. Sometimes the heroes are the main ones needing saving. Do me a favor. Be careful with your words. Even big men have insecurities and hurt that we carry. I'm learning to be okay with mine, well, at least on my good days.

TIMOTHY "URBAN THOUGHTS" MOORE

Sticks And Stones

They say: Sticks and stones
May break my bones
But words will never hurt me.

I was in class the next day after,
watching the clock tick-tocking,
remind me of my friend's arms
dangling after suicide.
Still swinging like holding time,
No one even noticed the tears just the snickers on my desk.

The homeless gentleman outside the store called out,
AYE, AYE let me get two dollars big dog!
Felt like he was cursing me.
Took me five seconds to unball my fists
and not hit him in the mouth.
But- I understood.
I smiled,
As big people do.

I've learned how to laugh off jokes,
even when they hurt.
I laugh cause like most,
He couldn't see the scars from behind the pounds,
Or the hurt behind the poems,
Or the weight of the stanzas.

AFTER THE RAIN FALLS

He couldn't see that the two dollars he was asking for
was the last of my paycheck
To give my daughter a roof and food.
I remember still being hungry three days later.
I wanted God to give me the strength of Lazarus to rise
back from this buffet
that my best friend paid for with good intentions.

I silently thanked my friend for placing a crack addict
in a trap house with nine pounds of white
and expecting me not to get high off of the supply of: Food.
I wonder which friend is going to help me wash my mouth out
after I vomit my guilt back unto this stage,
I mean toilet.

Three years ago, I literally starved my body
to the point of dying on the side walk for 7.4 seconds
Funny, don't remember the dying.
I do remember the sleep.
Was the first time, I remember not being hungry.
Food be both love and addiction,
Stressor and healer,
Allah, Oshun, and Jesus.
Science says the body needs food to survive,
Needs water to thrive. Ironic,
The very thing I need is my addiction.

I've survived suicide by slit wrists,
A gun shot that missed because I flinched,
And yet these calories be my biggest vice.
At suicide awareness meetings,

TIMOTHY "URBAN THOUGHTS" MOORE

I question daily whether I'm more survivor
Or victim. Addicted to the idea of dying.

Every time, I reach for the Pringles.
Just gotta eat one more.
I'm just now learning how to not eat one more.

The sun be tormentor
How it shines light on my body
Breaking the shadows, I'd rather walk in.
Let's kids in grocery stores point fingers.
Heard one call me the black Pillsbury dough boy. Once,
I almost laughed. Until I remembered,
That I had been through rehab for using my dough
To bury pills in this body.

Doctors name me: Special.
Question how I've survived to do these poems.
I told them I like to trim that truth.
Makes me feel better because
Black boys can't be insecure about weight.

We can't be sad bout burdens.
Ain't got no damn time to be mourning over no pounds.
Gotta be strong all the time.
Can't weigh others down
Cause Black boys can't cry
And Black men shole can't wail.

Last night- Had a poet ask me why I'm sweating?
Had a fan call me fly: for a fat guy.

AFTER THE RAIN FALLS

I wanted to tell them
That dressing sloppy
Makes me self-conscious.

These clothes are my make-up.
I tell myself that I'm not necessarily hiding.
I am concealing
Myself and these insecurities
And honestly- I've learned how to hide
smiles in suit coats, custom jeans, and funny t-shirts
with slogans that remind me not to cry at myself.

The Cymbalta is supposed to stop that
But it lifts my body temperature to hell.
I've gone through ribs broken from flipping cars,
Surgery repaired lungs to keep them inflated,
And mental illness.
When I say I breathe life into this poetry
I'm not lying.

This -
be my therapy and honestly,
I'd rather carry all this weight
than have you try to,

And break.

The Villain

An old silent foe:
Depression. A brother gone-
Boom! Heart drops again.

AFTER THE RAIN FALLS

When The Pandemic Came

When we breathe, we always think it will be forever.
Assume that our lungs will always be alive.
We acknowledge the living as if they will always be present
As if roses will forever be a sweet-smelling flower,
Or if ice cream will always be cold delights.

So when the pandemic came,
It became chaos.
Became disruption.
Became silence.
Stopped the music,
Of feet on concrete streets.
Made whisper of car honks.
Folded the "Hey, how are you?" into origami masks.

The silence came.
The not knowing came.
The isolation came.
The quiet of one's own worries
And hearts came.
The silence of questioning,
Can we endure; ourselves?
The losses mounted into the 100's
Then 1000's. Until,
Over half a million stars gathered in the sky as new constellations.

TIMOTHY "URBAN THOUGHTS" MOORE

For the first time,
I watched a friend die from afar
In the same city.
In a hospital, down the street from my home
Behind a glass that became his new apartment.
Across a distance that was less that an arm reach,
Yet, a continent away, in hazmat suits
Where all we could do was exchange
Glances. Through the windows,
When he died.
He died alone.
Buried alone.
No funeral was held that week.

Next week, my brother would have been 45.
He spent his whole life putting fires out.
Running into fiery buildings.
Putting on suits made to keep him safe.
Ironic, how now his lungs
Became filled with the only thing fire is afraid of:
Water.
I visit his gravesite every week.
We talk.
The grass and flowers know him intimately.
In his last moments, I am sure
Even the ground was confused,
As to how to bury such a beautiful flame.

This is the silence.
The moments of helplessness that divide.
When the pandemic came-

AFTER THE RAIN FALLS

Family, friends, and strangers who could be loves of our lives
Passed us by.
Behind masks
That we wore to pretend that we were doing okay,
We wore sorrow and fear gripped our smiles.
We learned to hide in plain sight,
And that is the silence.
That is the silence.
That is the...

Stardust

(For Rev. Ulysses "June" Jones III, my god-brother)

When we were little, we would stare at the sun.
At night, we would capture fireflies and pretend that we were catching stars.
As we grew, we learned their names Triangulum Astrale, Sirius, and Vega.
In College, we learned their purpose and what they are made of.
Wolf Rayets are the brightest of stars.
They can outshine entire galaxies.
Most are capable of blinding the sun.
Some are 330,000 times the size of Earth.
When they smile, you can feel their love over eternities away.
As older men, we learned how humans become carbon:
Become stardust.
Become angels-if they loved right here on Earth.
I am sure you were a Wolf-Rayet!
June- all massive and strong and big and hugs and love.
Sure, you be cousin to Scorpius or Polaris.

These special types of stars are rare.
When exhausted, they create a gravity disturbance.
Once they leave, their absence sends shockwaves through the universe.
The old ones would say Angels are crying,
When they would see the white streaks race across the sky.
Say Jesus be lighting Fireworks, giving us a show.

AFTER THE RAIN FALLS

Astronomers say when a Wolf-Rayet passes away that it becomes Supernova.
In one final burst, love brightens universes
The hood says that the brightest of stars burn the quickest.
Say be the good ones that go.
Tupac- 25, Dr. Martin Luther King- 39, Malcolm X- 40 and yeah you, **June-45**.
All stars who burned with everything they had to create light around them
Illuminated the darkness with a passion that God gave- **Jesus-33**

And so it was Light.
And so it was as much as.
June gave that he became star.
Became Light. Became Love. Became supernova.
Finally God, let his love guide us in the darkness.
Placed him right in the sky and now when we look outside our windows.
The brightest star reborn.
I am sure it is you because God always
Uses the best of us to light the way for others.
I am thankful to be reminded of you.
Every time I search the sky and look up, I will remember to be love.

TIMOTHY "URBAN THOUGHTS" MOORE

Absent Notes
(For Asha)

There are raindrops that never reach the ground.
Prayers or solemn attempts to give life,
Lost, splattered on concrete objects.
Ledges wet with disappointment or regret.
Areas never meant to become watered
From the wrong approaches and angles.

Communication fractures over time and distance.

Excused or unexcused notes from students
That I can't give to my one **daughter** who lives in Nashville
to excuse me from absence from your life
Or presence- in their lives.

These classrooms I teach in gather moments
that linger of memories,
That were never created with you.

I stare at the rain realizing that water only knows home.
Falls anyway. Even when skies are too far to reach
inside classrooms. When it rains
and I'm teaching. It becomes apparent
that a parent missing to one is found by many.
Ironic, how I have become more tornado
affecting everything around you but-
you. You called anyway and I missed it.

AFTER THE RAIN FALLS

The phone clicks over.
Voicemail knows your voice more than I do some days.
I stand frustrated in front of PowerPoints and handouts.
More educator than father most days,
More ground than rain on others. Longing,
Unwatered, connections of empty hugged
Arms outstretch dangling with 281 miles of space in between.
How many feet of highways traveled after work can be
multiplied to show love?
How much child support or gifts can be factored to show
sacrifice?

I wonder if she will ever know Moses fiery bush,
Or the joy of the prodigal father,
Or the miracle of just loving something
More than self, like I love her?

She stands in my arms.
Calls me father.
Sometimes, I wonder if it is just reflex
To my sentimental dad, I love you statements,
Or a vitriol response to my students,
Or just the truth of a daughter
That understands love more than her father does.

Maybe it is just the thought of how much I could love
If we could be more present
Or at least me-not be so absent.

She

She doesn't catch the sadness of thought/ or the slight twinge of fear/ that dangles upon my lips/ I hold my pain in when she says/ she's leaving/ I bury it deep/ so that all of my wishes/ won't burden her needs/ and it hurts/ part of me wants her to just see my heart/ yet I can't/ I love her/ and she needs to go/to be happy/again.

AFTER THE RAIN FALLS

For The Black Girls That Never Come Home

Breonna Taylor, I wish America would stop making Black Women, disappear.
Black folks line streets like audience just clapping and whooping loudly.
Black folks sit mourning. Watching the body while waiting on the spirit to return.

We gasp. Collective realizes that there is no magic in these Southern tricks:
We all are left silently growing in our rage. Wondering.
Why does America love the show but not the people in it?

Why does America love her body but not the soul it represents?
Is it for the magic...
...The Black girl magic?

See *Breonna Taylor.* **Hear** *Breonna Taylor.* **Say** *her name.* **Breonna Taylor** *was a 26-year-old healthcare professional who was fatally shot while sleeping inside her Louisville, Kentucky apartment. Three white plain-clothed officers of the Louisville Metro Police Department (LMPD) served a No-Knock Forced Entry on suspicion of drug dealing operations that was not properly served or searched. The boyfriend frightened by the break-in, fired one warning shot that was met with 32 shots in* *return. Six of those bullets struck Ms. Breonna Taylor with one bullet being the fatal shot that ended her life. None of the three police officers were charged with the homicide or with the murder. One police officer was charged but not due to the murder but for striking the wall. That police officer was charged and indicted for the bullets that struck the wall there by wanton endangerment of the next-door neighbors. Which is to say, a black woman's life is worth less than a wall of mud and paint according to those that uphold the law.*

The sadness in this story is so layered. Her body became, Sarah Baartman, placed on show for people to put on shirts with slogans about protecting Black Women. Protecting women became about looking cool versus doing the work to ask, What is/was/and will be needed? Some of that work includes checking men who do harm especially <u>some</u> White men who still fetishize a Black woman's curves but not her value in boardrooms, henceforth, the direct lack of matching salaries for equal work. Breonna Taylor's life and death in many ways became tokenized. Everything became a numbing spray to her value. The truth is- this is how Black women have been mistreated in our struggle for freedom of Black and Brown bodies.

In the movement, Black women have led and equally supported men. You think of two of arguably the strongest advertised Black leaders and you immediately see the counterweight of strength. Reverend Dr. Martin Luther King, Jr., had the courageous and meticulous Coretta Scott King to push through all the tough moments of working through systematic oppression in the South. Malcolm X had the brilliant and compassionate Betty Shabazz to brain storm his ideas and think through the macro issues of his campaign. These women were powerful leaders who chose to follow. When Black women have their issues where they should and ought to be leaders of, men, come into those spaces and even from follower roles try to usurp leadership to push to the front. I think this is the exact backwards of how Black women work in ally ship. It is such a beautiful notion of sacrifice and follow through.

As a cis heterosexual male, I will never know how it feels to give birth. For this direct reason, I strongly feel that I have no place to tell a female (woman) what they can and can't do with their womb. I can ally. I can empathize and have sympathy for that specific issue but for me, it is an issue that should be left to those directly affected. This is to not say that the burden becomes solely to women. I disagree with that notion. The burden lays on all; however, the voices, faces, and the frame of leadership should be honored and respected with the same enthusiasm as if a cis male was leading.

Black women are too often voiceless characters in a sitcom that bares their name but not their voice. As we protest, the need to normalize Black women being honored as more than help meet in this struggle is past due time to be respected. Our women deserve to be protected whether they are at our shoulder, one step behind or 100 steps out in front leading. For me, it is calling out people that look like me: 1. Black males (men) specifically to step back equally as we step up. 2. A call for all men to recognize the sacrifices of our Black Women (Womxn) and 3. Support with equal vigor the responsibilities of roles. My hope is to ensure that Breonna Taylor's death isn't sensationalized or becomes nothing more than a passing moment that stood as an afterthought to other Black deaths due to police brutality. Let her loss linger upon your lips until they part in a controlled rage to drive the changing of laws to protect the next Breonna Taylor. In essence, I am tired of watching all the names pile up at death's door. Black women bodies deserve more than empty magic tricks where the magician claims the support and love is coming but never produces the idea to sustenance. Black Woman (Womxn) bodies deserve to go to sleep and not have to worry about waking up safe. My youngest, Imani, is 2 years old. I pray for her every night when she clutches my chest. I pray that she is always safe. Black Women deserve to go to sleep and not have to worry.

Black Girl Magic

(For Breonna Taylor)

I wish America would stop making Black women-disappear.
Black folks sit mourning, watching the body, while waiting on the spirit to return.
We collectively realize there is no magic in those tricks:
We are left silently growing in our rage,
Wondering-why does America like to harm our women?
Is it for the magic?

TIMOTHY "URBAN THOUGHTS" MOORE

Graffiti and Teddy Bears

Nations all over the world grieve their dead
In Mexico, Day of the Dead
In Japan, Paper folded into beautiful swans
Or lotus to carry ancestors along water
And yes, in America,
More specifically the hood,
We have our markers on light poles.
Teddy bears with arms stretched up to Heaven,
As if they know how to pray.
We cry. Balloons release,
Floating off on the psalms of the present.

Behind graffiti walls,
I've seen murals of teddy bears
resurrected for my black boys.
I've learned to sing broken songs.
Psalms of mothers sung,
Prayers by the elders,
Background bass being both bottom
and grounding for humans who mourn in pews.
Oh, how the choir fills the room.
Rev preaching the Gospel.
Fathers holding mothers.
Friends collapsing into friends.

AFTER THE RAIN FALLS

Murals painted into memories.
Babyface cheek bones part.
Laughter: mixture of giggle
And equal part full belly chuckle.
Backdrops of trumpets blaring for the forgotten.

Sirens have become staccato symphony
Souls lifted to heaven by song
My God, look at the palms raised
While pastor reads over the body
Though I walk through the shadow of death
The black boys buried beyond
Bass drums and backbeats brought down by the timbre of a cop's brass

We've learned not to fear the siren song
It has become so common
That we have stopped marching
And we sing along

The lost boys be found in Heaven.
God bless us still living.
Hashtag our sorrows.
Hieroglyph our memories.
Let stars be both story and connector.

Let them tell our stories between the dashes.
As they look down to see us gathered,
Between the Graffiti and the Teddy Bears.

TIMOTHY "URBAN THOUGHTS" MOORE

Twenty-Three

This poem be for
My boys
My guys
The bruhs
The homies
And all who practiced Jordan's fadeaways
to the beat of flickering street lights

God bless those that lowered the rim to 6 feet
Ironic how mentioning 6 feet now
Brings different feelings
Doesn't bring the same smiles of mobs to cheer
But angry marches at the latest hashtag

Before we understood the difference
Between sorrow and joy
We flew through the air mimicking "23"
Tongues out
Defying gravity
Turning our little brothers
Into Scottie with the Fro
Legs stretched out
Tomahawk one-handed
Dunks from the free throw line
Relentlessly
Creating beauty from ugly

AFTER THE RAIN FALLS

This be for us - Black boys
Who found the Magic in letting our imaginations be
The Bird in the corner taking flight over Kareem's hook shot
This be for my black boys
who are worth more than their contracts
Could ever pay for grieving moms

Question:
"What if SportsCenter broadcast the stats of all the lynched black boys?"

This poem be for all of us
The found and forgotten
The black boy bodies buried and broken,
Borne brand new between basketball
Found in the beaten chalk lines.

I always wondered when we find Heaven

Will God forgive us for air dunking on halos

We pray
Hands clasped for the other
Knowing that at any given time
Any given moment
The clock could strike twelve
And our fairytale
Could be ripped out
Burned to by twelve
This poem be
For my boys

TIMOTHY "URBAN THOUGHTS" MOORE

My guys
My men
The son I never had

And all who all practiced living
Before we learned to be afraid
Of the blue lights
Before we learned that some blue lights hang
Over bodies
And not rims
Before some gained wings
Before MVP trophies

This be for us
The forgotten
The lost
The black boys
Black men
My guys
The homies
My bruhs
And all who practiced Jordan's fadeaways
To the beat of flickering streetlights

May we all make it home safe
Before the shot clock runs out

AFTER THE RAIN FALLS

My First Love Letter

I loved you.

She be beauty of the universe.
I watched her hold the cosmos
In the twinkle of her eyes,

And yet, she sits.
Head down, contemplating.
Is my dark skin as ugly as her classmates say?

Years, before I loved her
Wish I could have loved her enough
To make her realize her worth beyond my poetry
Or support that she didn't have to change,
Anything. She was perfect.

Growing up all the boys wanted her.
But I was slicker than Rick.
Rocking my Kangol with my black and white 3 stripe,
Thick gold Cuban link chains,
Listening to L. L. Cool J's "Rock the Bells"
Or "I Need Love"
Cause that's what I'd do.
Sit in the room,
Lock the door
And wait for you to sing to me.

TIMOTHY "URBAN THOUGHTS" MOORE

My mom mad at the noise
But you were beautiful to me.
I vowed we'd grow old together.
Hold hands. Sit in the park
After dark and take the long walks
Jill talked about.

When I got older,
I took her to Egypt.
Watched the Great Pyramids
Deconstruct themselves backwards into the sand
Cause they didn't want to be compared
To her.

Watched the sun cause an eclipse with the moon
So that neither would have to share
The responsibility of matching her light.
She was beautifully classy.

Until one day, I noticed something different.
Her skirt was hiked up and her speech was different.
Profanity laced expletives flowing like the Mississippi.
I worried she was changing. Tried to talk to her.
Until finally I saw her, for her.
Rose colored glasses off.

She got out of a tinted-out black Camaro sitting on 30-inch floater rims
A daughter p-popping on hand stands in her left hand
And a son banging gang signs in her right hand.
I was confused.

AFTER THE RAIN FALLS

Yelled out for her.
But she said, "I couldn't compete anymore."
My affections couldn't match the dollars.
Decided long ago to allow the bands to make her dance
Than let love keep her in a good rhythm.

After all we'd been through,
I couldn't understand, why she left to date Mumble Rap.
Hip-hop I thought you loved me.
Hip-hop I thought you loved me.
Thought we would grow old together.
Now I just turn on the radio
Turn on the oldies
And remember how we used to be.

Sincerely,
Poetry

TIMOTHY "URBAN THOUGHTS" MOORE

Invisible Hoodies

When I grew up my father told me the golden rule:
No Hoodies
He said every boy like me had an invisible one on
Made them unnecessary to wear

When I grew up my father never let me play with a toy gun.
Never let me believe that they were fun
and no matter how many times my boys would offer a reason,
Dad would claim treason.
He would say no color tipped black chromed gun
whether orange yellow or pink toy
would ever be made safe enough for his little black boy
to carry -so no son- you can't have one.

Mama then offered my friends politely a cookie & the door.
I would pout on the floor.
Not tall or wise enough to understand,
I'd complain.

Until now, see now, I've seen enough urban lynchings by bullets flying
dividing families into the living
Versus the dying
To understand that my father's rules still apply.

AFTER THE RAIN FALLS

In a grocery store looking at a little boy who plays with toy guns,
I choke on my own tears.
I wonder if that black boy will make it home to even play with it.
Remembering my father's rules,
My Father's black boy rules that gather the sounds of CNN broadcasts of
The murdered –muffled screams in between back seats of police cars
handcuffed to pleas of don't move nigger.
Pow!
What you reaching for?
Pow!
Look forward, not Black.

Rules that have become so habitual that they seem to
No longer be his or twitter mentions
But my own hash tags **#BlackBoyRules.**
Stand tall. Shoulders back. Head up.

1. Upon entering a corner grocery store, never keep your hands inside your pockets.
Hands inside pockets hide intentions,
Give fearful imaginations, motive.

2. Greet the cashier with a Hi! how are you?
Wave.
Smile.
Wave again.

TIMOTHY "URBAN THOUGHTS" MOORE

Give distance between politeness and cashiers imagined threat.

Beware the label they attach with hip-hop images.
Be pronounced and diligent with your greeting.
Speak proper English, boy.
Don't dare be man enough or be to bold to speak in your native tongue.

Beware black boys of the trouble unseen or untold.

It is in the fold of hoodies that blackness seems most dangerous
so make every situation around you light.

3. Never buy skittles or tea without visible receipt.
In darkness, they combine without under moonlight
to become monsters on walls in the dark.
And, people fear monsters.

Gather black boys. Gather under the rules of your fathers
and be careful black boys so you can return home
to your father's arms by choice
and not casket.
Beware black boys.
These are the #BlackBoyRules
To survive to become Men.

AFTER THE RAIN FALLS

Black Diamonds

Black boys be beautifully crafted black diamonds
Rare in sight and touch
Black mothers hold sons like prisms hold elegance
Watching God kiss them equally with Light

We watch black boys grow into Black men
Rare in sight and touch
Black mothers hold sons like skies hold stars
Watching God bless them equally with love

We hear Black boys make song of psalms
Rare in sight and touch
Black mothers hold sons like treble hold bass
Watching God make joyous music out of their lives

Black boys be beautifully crafted Black Diamonds
Black boys be handsome stars in skies
Black boys be jazz and blues and all the good notes of songs
Black boys be loved by black moms

Yeah, Black boys be loved by black moms
And don't you ever forget that black boys be loved
We be loved

TIMOTHY "URBAN THOUGHTS" MOORE

Before We Grew Up

Do you remember?
Do you remember when the best toy was a box?
We jump in with our socks on.
Pretend to be airplane pilots and go wherever we wanted to go
Everywhere but here.
Get out of the box.
Flip it on its' side.
Attach a coat hanger and pretend that it was the color television
That we didn't have yet
That has been coming for like the last five years from layaway

Do you remember how it was to just to have fun?
To mob up to the corner with your boys with a dollar to the candy lady
And come back with 99 cause you always lost one on the way back?
How it was to play hopscotch, double-dutch, bounce the ball, catch a jack
And to run around playing cops and robbers?
Ain't it funny how back then nobody wanted to be the robber?
Now after so many bruised bodies of beaten blacks, boys
Would rather pretend to be the robbers.

Do you remember how Native Americans use to be the bad guys?

AFTER THE RAIN FALLS

Before history taught us that they weren't the invaders or the villains?
But the Natives- who loved?
Do you remember how we use to go to church?
How we used to come to church?
It was serious business dressed to the nines.
Early. Never just on time or after tithes and offering?
Do you remember how grandma used to check
The length of girls' skirts by making sure they fell below fingertips?
Do you remember when the ushers would come and take your phones?
Grandpa be like, "Pay attention, the pastor's teaching."
Remember how we used to have our face deep in the books of the Bible
Instead of comments on Facebook?
Remember when church was about work in the community
And not likes, stunts or retweets?
When scars on knees were indications of how much you prayed last week?

Do you remember the last time you were broken
Begging God for one more chance from whatever vice
That brought you to church that week?
But once you forgot you stopped, coming?
Now you been missing since New Year's Eve?
Do you remember what it's like to be black and in church
Loving God, as if God meant more than being smart and Hotep
And Black as if God actually existed?
Do you remember faith?

TIMOTHY "URBAN THOUGHTS" MOORE

Forgiveness?
What it's like to forgive?

Remember community?
We used to love the community.
We used to be in love with our community.

AFTER THE RAIN FALLS

Dear Son

Dear son,
I never realized that half of my soul would be so cheap.
I'm writing this letter because I never got the chance to say goodbye.
Truth is, when I was 19, I was a coward willing to overlook the signs of your mother's pregnancy.

My granddad said, "You got to graduate"
Already excusing my actions as if my future was more valuable than hers.
As if, my graduating to fatherhood wasn't what our community needs more of.
I chose to give money to your mother so that I could be free of accountability.

Ain't that the story of Pinocchio? Me,
A fake boy pretending to be a real man,
Refusing to grow up,
Trapping his son in Neverland.
Lost boys everywhere. Father may as well be called Peter Pan.
Creating fairytales while revealing realities
Of my boyish laziness of complacency and shaky work history
Which left your mother open to question the possibility of her security.

TIMOTHY "URBAN THOUGHTS" MOORE

Son, I lied to you and myself too often.
As if, half of my soul wasn't connected to the purchase.
But, how do you give half of her soul
And all her black girl magic back after an abortion?

On the way to the clinic, I prayed the Doctors would be gentle.
Research said the process would be painless due to medicine
But the question I couldn't find an answer to was
What numbs the soul before deliverance?
God, where were my angels to protect me from my devils?
Where were they to tell me that those 30 pieces of silver would make me-
my son's Judas.

I'm reminded in the quiet of the room that they say sons are like their father's.
So did you fight to stay in?
Did you hold on to her ovaries using them as handlebars refusing to let go?
Did you KungFu kick the doctor on the way out?
Throw a finger sign at the nurse?
Pretend to be Sampson.
Try to grow hair long enough to fight?
Did you fight?
Did you fight like I should have fought for you?

For that brief moment as machines took turns creating an automatic heartbeat,
Suctioning you from your mother's womb.
Your soul transitioning into heaven
I questioned: Should my name have been Mourning Father, Mr.

AFTER THE RAIN FALLS

Policeman or Zimmerman?
What makes me different?
When I stopped a black boy from growing up just the same?

Sitting in the uncomfortable silence that sat in between me
and your mother's blood on the ride home.
I remember the stench of piss as I soiled my pants
At the thought that I am half of the man that you already were.
I carried her from the car-
into the house.
Your mother painting-
My arms,
Stained glass church windows, crimson dyed reflections of your
broken smile.
My arms,
Painted memories of you in my heart that I will never forget.

We sat quietly in a distance that we never learned how to close.
Became strangers in a house that was no longer home.
And buried grief into too many arguments over a son
that never came back.
No matter how many prayers we prayed
And God knows we prayed,
For you,
to come back.

Sincerely,
Your father who wasn't strong enough to say,
"Welcome home."

TIMOTHY "URBAN THOUGHTS" MOORE

Birthday Candles

My mother had me on her birthday.
She never lets me forget.
This year we celebrated another birthday- My mom and I.
My mom bragging about the cake she baked and that I was an okay gift
To give herself as if my dad didn't really help.

The air will be filled with the aroma of caramel.
People will congratulate me and her.
Music will play but none with curse words.
Mama only like words that speak life.

My mom's laughter will be the only music that I need though.
Mama's laughter be Dizzy Gillespie meets Billie Holiday
Charlie Parker and Jay-Z forming a trio with Erykah Badu-
Yeah, that cool.

At 16, my mom's voice marked time to the melody of her black boy
not being gifted teddy bears by chalk lines in the hood.
So proud that high school had embraced a black boy with open arms and not caskets.

At 18, it increased in volume to highlight that I actually became a man.

AFTER THE RAIN FALLS

That God blessed your birthday wish to close my slit wrist to celebrate, 19.
I hid them under my long sleeves but I know you knew
Cause you always kissed my forehead then my wrists.

God must have heard you and refused to leave me alone
He sent my godbrothers as angels.
They held them until, I could lie to you again.
That I was fine and college is going great, mom.

At 21 –Mama, your voice became symphony of a song
that your boy escaped the pipeline to prison.
The cuffs had fallen off.
Free as a man,
The walls came tumbling down.

I wonder if Samson had a mama like you would he ever have fallen for Delilah?
Then I realized that even Mama's couldn't heal all heartache.
It was the one birthday I spent lamenting in bed.
Divorced and heartbroken.

You ignored my pleas to be left alone and brought cake, anyway.
At 36 - it marked time to the orchestra of me being worried about the fact that
Mama - I've survived depression enough times to become depressed all over again,
That since God refuses to take me,
That there will be a time when I blow out the candles
wishing for you back.

TIMOTHY "URBAN THOUGHTS" MOORE

And how am I supposed to be joy on those birthdays,
Or happy for your laughter,
Or this cake?
How am I supposed to brag about the gift when the giver ain't there?
Then I will read this poem.

I will speak you back into life.
I will laugh.
I will remember that Mama gave me life
And that life ain't meant for crying.

Some gifts such as time
are meant to be enjoyed.
I will laugh. I will hug.
I will love. I will enjoy the memories of your laughter, Mama
And all the times we blew the candles out,
Together.

Chapter Three:

The Awakening - After The Rain Falls

After the rain falls, the clouds part.
The sun comes out.
The irony is, it is the same world.
The only difference is your perspective.

So, let me get this right, #IssaSnack?

*According to Dictionary.com, a **snack** is a noun that is one of three following definitions:*

1. a small portion of food or drink or a light meal, especially one eaten between regular meals.
2. a share or portion.
3. Australian Slang for something easily done.

Do you ladies truly want to be a snack?

Do you truly want to be an item that is just something to do in-between your mate's true love and their exes? We are so quick in this dating age to be used and discarded. We have made it acceptable behavior to Netflix and chill with the intent to just hit and quit. When we lessen our value to the expected outcome then we become snacks. We become easily attained. Worse, we become easier to consume then discarded in the trash bin of dating waste. I am not slut shaming by any means. I know in all things we have free will and choice to sleep with whom we wish but if you act in a manner, then be sure of the consequences and the following issues that follow. Don't go buy a hamburger and expect it to taste like a filet mignon with a buttered lobster tail. Don't cry when Little Ant, Eric or Mac Mark gets locked up or has two side chicks with nine babies. He told you from the start and showed you from the first conversation that he thought you were a snack.

A portion?
Don't confuse being a willing portion to being a side portion. Nowadays, the black community is embracing the polyamorous or (PolyAm Lifestyle). It is nothing new. Do a quick history check and you will see most countries and religions even Christianity embraced the PolyAm lifestyle. Many of God's best warriors and men had multiple wives/lovers. I can go into that but that is a whole other commentary. A willing portion is a choice to be an addition to and a main attraction. A snack is an easily consumed and quickly discarded option often with no nutritional value. What am I saying? Stop being a snack and wondering why your relationships are coming up short? Your expectations are too small. I want my woman to be a whole farm, a supermarket chain, a never-ending waterfall that brings me life.

Easily done?
More than 10% of your encounters (and that is an extremely high number) should not be easily attained flings. One, it just isn't healthy! Have you seen the STD rates in Memphis lately or the nation? Scary stuff, indeed. Second, your body is not a playground for you to litter on. Stop accepting boys and trying to turn them into men. Gathering spirits in your yoni like a cemetery and wondering why you can't give birth to your dreams. You aren't a mother raising a grade school child. Stop packing snacks to occupy their time.

Domestic Violence
Domestic violence is a real thing. People think that domestic violence is limited to hitting or almost dying. It is that! Definitely, that is domestic violence and wrong but it is also allowing the

mental degradation of yourself to become normal. It's the lessening of your worth to accept him calling you anything other than your name -while he drives your car, eats your food, pays his bills with your money, and disrespects your living space. We make excuses about how good they treat us during the short time. I mean they respect snack time, Right? .

I know that it's only a term; however, for a poet with 3 daughters: Words matter. I need my three daughters to know that being a snack is not cool. I don't ever want them to grow up thinking that they are snacks when they are immensely powerful women beyond measure. My daughters are not snacks and you aren't either.

AFTER THE RAIN FALLS

Just Beautiful

I told her that her roundness was: Just Beautiful.
She couldn't believe that I could see beauty in her fullness.
She had become used to guys wanting to be her gym partner
Instead of trying to be her husband.
Men giving her demands of if you could lose a few more pounds- you'd be a dime.
Time after time men made her beauty relative to a number on a scale.
So, she never learned how to value herself well,
Woman, you should know that you are perfectly crafted artistry
And not a guy's fetish for a BBW lifestyle party.
Evidence that God used Extra clay to balance out your personality.
Baby, I get it. Your curves bare the burdens others did not have the grace to handle
Should you decide to lose the weight?
Do it for you and not to measure up to the height of a hater's insecurities.

She told me that she was no video vixen.
In her mind, being thin seems more of a curse than blessing,
More indictment than perfection,
And more falsely injected curves in awkward places
To fulfill more of a Barbie fantasy than a black girl reality.
Baby! Shouts of gain a little weight becomes average outbursts from men.

TIMOTHY "URBAN THOUGHTS" MOORE

You'd be stout and perfect.
As if her image is more coffee mug than person.
The angles of your body are equal to the precision of The Great pyramids of GIZA.
Each line and curve for a specific purpose,
You are far from ever being worthless.
So, model in poise and grace
That you are always just beautiful.

Show the Beauty in your muscles.
If you didn't look so buff,
I'd cuff: You.
As if, he could lift half of your weight
Or run with the same pace and desire not to be late.
Each muscle anchors the dedication to make sure your body is a temple.
Each dimple a reminder that this earth is temporary.
I stand witness to the sweat and tears that you put in
Each push up, pushing down the criticism of the weak.

You brilliantly lift Black boys
Breaking your back to make them men.
Because of a lack of us, men.
You had to be strong.
Making it clear that God's first woman: Eve
Had to be Black.
Must have been Black
To birth a community from a single rib.
Making something from nothing
While the family grows strong.

AFTER THE RAIN FALLS

Yea you, you beautiful one,
We all have come from your womb.
You are our mothers and daughters.
Our next generation of melanin.
For black is not the absence of light
But the gathering of all light to a visible point.
We are in awe of black butterflies birthing black angels to fly.
So be-
Just beautiful Black girl.
Be just beautiful Black woman.
Be, just beautiful.
And remember you are just beautiful,
indeed.

Secrets

My tongue is a traitor.
I wish it could hold unto my secrets.
It betrays my heart to her ears.

AFTER THE RAIN FALLS

I Loved Once

Heartbroken
Before I lost
I thought I had it all
Now I see that I was already losing her
You see, me
a mirage of a king
more like the court jester
a villain playing in his own movie, no hero

I'm the empty reflection of the sun
casting shadows on a loves empty desert
Long forgotten how the flowers grow
Petals don't form as easily as likes would on Twitter
Touch we've forgotten-we text
I've forgotten how water taste
Dying so long this heart doesn't beat anymore
I spent my whole adult life giving ghosts the remnants of me
Spread my soul between women that never loved me
no matter how much I loved them
giving my poetry between the sheets
but how do you find the stanzas of your spirit
when you've lost God's pen so he can't write you back

Tears fill pages
These cool poems hold my truth hostage
Hiding behind mics

TIMOTHY "URBAN THOUGHTS" MOORE

Inspiring couples in relationships
of images I barely remember
Can someone tell me what love looks like
I've been trying to paint the image
but the canvas of her heart is paint resistant
I been trying to find out how to heal a broken heart
but how do you pick up the pieces to a puzzle
of what love should look like
when you never saw the image on the box of life

Been too busy trying to make temporaries: wives
paying the cost of being the perfect man for a night
Till the day comes: no vampire
But blade cuts at my heart strings
Not day walker enough to heal before the next victim
professing poems in places where love songs go silent
broken notes of lyrics that my heart can't sing
I bring myself broken before audiences
Wearing the mask as Dunbar did
Not understanding why I relate more to the cage Maya wrote
than the bird- good at trapping things
Not so good at freeing them
Vibrations upon the metal
that encloses my heart

You see the poet
but don't see the worries of pretending to be
a man you never truly wanted
I've found myself more faithful to self

AFTER THE RAIN FALLS

or a dollar rather than becoming a husband
You see the lover
but you don't see the hurt
You ask me why I am so cold
Well baby I been trying too long
to warm myself with women
That I've forgotten where my spiritual thermostat is

Rather watch my heart die than revive it
honestly, I almost died in love once
her silence resembled death
conversations lost in translation
we argued over my inability to love her correctly
each party blaming the other for the tears we shared

who caused them
me
you
us
my mind quietly filling voids left in kisses
by lusts desires,

I pray that my poison does not keep infecting my soul
my toxicity changes love's potency
breaking the pure
I envy those that see the beauty in my brokenness
cause my mirror no longer reflects the beauty of myself
but it **must**
cause every mirror deserves to hold the image of being loved

at least once

Please excuse me beautiful future
If I flinch when you say you could love me
cause I'm trying to remember how to love myself
enough to stay
long enough to learn how to love you
Like I finally learned how to love myself

#MeToo

Dear Rapists and Apologists,

My daughter Iyanla asked me, "Dad, what is #MeToo about?" I told her that #MeToo is a movement to draw awareness towards sexual assault, sexual harassment, and rape of people- specifically but not limited to women. I told her that men and women get raped every day. I told her that men and women assault others every day. I told her that #MeToo is primarily an effort to draw attention to the ugly #RapeCulture that is driving music, movies, and society.

I told Iyanla, that the #MeToo movement is not just a pretty hashtag but a request started by an African-American woman as a direct statement to oust rape culture and the supporting apologists that contribute to rape and assault. I told her that 1 out of 4 of her friends will most likely be raped or assaulted in their lifetime according to statistics. I told her that there is often a sense of shame for rape victims to come forward because people do not believe them and treat them as suspects and not victims before doing due research or investigation. I told her people will slut shame, grab, molest, fondle, and forcibly violate bodies because they dress a certain way. I told her that men specifically have a duty to protect all women and all beings on this earth. I told her that action of protection is different from a man being controlling. I told her love is not sexist or gender assumptions. I told her that we have to teach men and people NOT TO RAPE;

instead of promoting, misogynistic theorems on how women and people SHOULD NOT be raped.

I told her that I pray for her each day and night that she is not 1 of the 4. I told her this is why I taught you how to throw a jab, a straight, and a groin kick. I told her this is why I taught you how to escape being tied up. I told Yani this is why I bought her mace, a taser and will buy her a gun when she is legal to carry. I told her that I wish I didn't have to. I told her that I don't want her to ever have to post #MeToo.

I told her #MeToo should make men want to post that they understand and empathize. More men should post in support but that a lot of men have embraced unapologetically a culture of indulging in this American misogynistic, euro-centric patriarchy of a society that would rather excuse the actions of rapist as: young males under hormones, accidents, or too close to call. Some men would rather have it excused as funny jokes and memes in their circles. Statements by rappers for how women should act- i.e. Rick Ross (Rape culture-type statements that we endorse by buying his music.)

But where are my brothers? I think the one thing that can be done is to acknowledge and stand up when a brother is doing wrong. We have seen it. When you see it, call it out and protect; instead of, damage.

I sincerely don't want women or female gender identifying to feel as if I am taking light the movement by acknowledging men who post #MeToo. Even though, I know a few men that were raped well outside of prison walls in communities that we call ours. I once had a student call me. When I visited him at his home after the call, there were police cars and officers supporting him as they carried his body in. He sat silently on the edge of his front porch. He told me of how three grown men beat, robbed, then raped him. Ending his torture by sodomizing him with a broom handle. I asked him why he called me first instead of his family? He said they were going to ask him to pray for healing. He said that I would know how to press charges, go to the police, speak out, and take action. He said that he will pray later but he needed to "do" now. I know that #MeToo is about men, also. Hopefully, those men can find space to support the #MeToo movement while creating a separate hashtag that includes men and men identifying people as to not draw or deflect attention away from a much-needed conversation about rape.

We laugh it off. We joke at the unwanted grabs. We poke fun at each other's hurt. We allow others to violate safe spaces and out others. We throw around jokes of ugly words identifying things or actions. Take it. Take whatever, however and be grateful. Well, how? How do we stand so grateful of a society that promotes rape culture and rewards the rapist? I ask my men who stand by our ladies to love them, protect them, offer an ear and listen to their truths and stories without judgement so you can see how to help repair the damage. I challenge each man that reads this to use the hashtag #RealMenAsk. Or create your own to show that we are listening and more importantly than listening that we are willing to join in the fight against rape culture.

This essay is for my daughters. If ever- Then I will believe and fight for you because a Real Man should. We (men) should ask:

TIMOTHY "URBAN THOUGHTS" MOORE

What have you been through? How can I love you? How can I be love to you? Ask for consent and wait for a YES. Make consent the norm. They should understand your answers, listen and stop if there is ever a "No." We have to respect, protect, and love our women all the time.

AFTER THE RAIN FALLS

Chameleon

Fact: Chameleons can change their colors. They have special cells with a chemical called melanin that helps to literally allow the chameleon to blend in with their surroundings.

Opinion: I believe that he thought that if he beat her red that she would be able to hide her colors of pain by the stop signs her friends kept trying to give her.

Poem: She became a chameleon changing her colors to make him appear handsome.
Learned how to match her face to the red of his knuckles.
She became more punching bag than lover.
More abused than loved.
More him than her.
She forgot that the beauty of her skin was from within.
Her melanin coded by God.
When she'd pray for him to remember her beauty within.
He was in lust devil worshipping.
He'd comfort her after hitting her
by telling her that he prayed for her, too.

She forgot that the Devil could quote scripture and pray also.
Fact is, he wasn't praying for her.
As much as he was preying on her.
By keeping her beauty hostage, captive to the makeup
That helped her camouflage her brokenness
Into his

TIMOTHY "URBAN THOUGHTS" MOORE

She learned how to apply Fenty.
Fenty leave.
Fenty love myself.
Fenty fight back
But instead she just grew accustomed to making plenty of excuses.

She began to see nothing other than the floor she painted red.
The blood - staining bathroom tiles.
I would get calls at midnight-meeting her at her lowest.
Find her nailed to her own cross she'd bear with reasons
As to why she could be Mother Mary
And birth a miracle of him being born a new man.

In the drawer, the Bible, would shake to and fro.
Her body hitting the wall.
She'd pray to Jesus for another day to breathe,
But when granted the blessing of survival,
She'd forgive with her next granted breath.
She became too much chameleon and too less woman.

I loved her as a friend until she remembered that she could shed her skin.
I held her in my arms to remind her that all men aren't monsters.
Her skin started to reform, her melanin capturing the essence of the sun.
Black Queens circled her.
Sharing their crowns until hers became polished enough to wear again.
I watched them drum circles of conversations.

AFTER THE RAIN FALLS

Healing hearts over cocktails and hugs,
Her feet became rooted,
Clutching into mother earth,
She began to see him for him

And not for the value of what he could be.
She remembered that Lois never jumped out of windows to save Superman.
So when he came she told him with her mother's tongue:
Her name.
He grew afraid.
He knew that he could not battle the sharpness of her teeth or her claws.
She shed her skin of victim
And hit back with all that she had and he left.

She called the cops.
I came over that night tired of masking,

But...
We did not use the mascara, blush or glue
We did not camouflage or hide
We stood.

She stood.
In her new skin.

Didn't you know that chameleons always learn how to survive?

TIMOTHY "URBAN THOUGHTS" MOORE

Dear Black Men:
That's Gay

"Black men struggle with masculinity so much. The idea that we must always be strong really presses us all down - it keeps us from growing." -Donald Glover

Dear Black Men,
Donald Glover once wrote that, "Black men struggle with masculinity so much. The idea that we must always be strong really presses us all down - it keeps us from growing." This quote played in my head when Moonlight won the Oscar. Too often in a black male's life, our masculinity has been defined by being "not gay." Don't play with Barbie dolls, cook food in the kitchen, clean just enough to be-clean, and the most damaging "Don't Cry- Man Up." As if men are incapable of crying, we were supposed to never shed a tear. I cried watching Moonlight. It is a magnificent film of conflict, triumph, self-discovery, blackness, and masculinity.

In the African-American community, we often struggle with being accepted and having equal rights. Yet, we chastise and ostracize African-American homosexual males while glorifying homosexual females. Nas X is outcast while Cardi B and others can shoot similar content with praise and approval. Simultaneously, we continue to create running jokes of "That's Gay." As if being gay was some type of weakness or some type of kryptonite that if black males were around it too long that we would instantaneously die.

AFTER THE RAIN FALLS

I've always thought of myself as an open-minded individual even after growing up in a small, all Black town of Tuskegee where Baptist preaching on a Sunday is life. I've always considered myself masculine and heterosexual; however, during Moonlight, my own biases came forward. I had gone with a thought that it was a coming-to-age story of a young boy turned drug dealer turned man which is part of the storyline. As the story progressed, I found myself uncomfortable. I started to realize that my own biases were coming out and I wanted to get up and walk out. This was "gay" and the societal image of a "straight man" watching it in the South was uncouth. Thoughts that I can't be in here watching this came up. The stench of my hypocrisy that I teach kids every day to confront to love each other, respect each other, and to accept other's differences smacked me square in the face. Now when the teacher is tested, I was failing. I sat down. I rooted myself to finish the movie to become what I wish of my students become-courageous in the face of adversity and self-questioning.

The acting and storyline kept me there wanting to understand why I was so bothered. As the movie progressed, I found myself in a battle of sympathy versus empathy. As a heterosexual Black male, I could sympathize with the struggle of identity and being physically assaulted. I was jumped once in a rival school after a football game. The feelings of anger, vengeance, fear, and vulnerability are real. The next week, I remember feeling alone often as I was in classrooms labeled gifted. Labeled with one of the highest I.Q.'s in some of the schools I attended. I became a guinea pig of sorts in honors classes, Clue, and special classes where I was the only black boy in some spaces. I was a current day popular minstrel show for school administration to show off, "Oooooh, look at the black boy think and dance," while greeting strangers for the school. Parents, family and a whole community labeling what you should be before you even know who you are.

As the movie went on, tears welled in my eyes. I sympathized with the main character who was a homosexual male with the triple burden of being Black, American, and homosexual. It's hard enough to be male and Black. I never thought about the added third layer of others. I will never feel that tri-level of conflict of just wanting your own family of blackness to love you. Moonlight establishes this burden so eloquently in this film because it makes you see for just an instance how dangerous being Black and gay is. I started to hurt and feel great empathy for Chiron "Little" as he struggled through poverty. The only difference between me and Little was that my mother and father loved me so much that I was never truly conscious of how poor we were until I was much older in high school noticing the difference of our clothes to our neighbor's name brands.

As Chiron grew up learning to adapt and blend, I understood my journey that took me on a road similar to the prodigal son paradigm in which I took to the streets for my gold that I thought I deserved. Vowing never to be poor again, I set out on a course to blend and adapt to become tougher to fit in with the boys in my high school and younger years in college. The deeds of my youth were many and I'm not proud of them or the consequences. I understand death too well from watching friends shot and killed, the burden of two attempted and one successful suicide that left me flat lined and brought back.

Finally, Chiron "Black", shows the love, forgiveness of self and others, redemption and knowledge that comes with finally realizing who and what you are. It was then I wept. Some of my best friends are gay. They are honest. They are some of the best poets, singers, and a comic that I know in Memphis and yet I let society choose for me how I positioned them in relation to me in public. Today, I unpack the embedded biases of my youth to grow up. Moonlight is a beautiful film. It does not question masculinity any more than being gay makes you less of a man. What Moonlight manages is to force you to come to terms with what your internal ideas of masculinity are.

I am proud to say that I understand that I have some biases in me that need working on to allow me to mature as a man. There is a necessity in life to mature. We can't stay the same in boyish thinking that our masculinity is tied to our external sex organs alone. That we as black men in this society must be tough robotic creatures to bear the brunt of pain without shedding a tear or admitting that we need love. We all deserve love. We all deserve to understand that someone else's choices are theirs alone to have the right to choose to define their own masculinity and sexuality.

I stand firm in my belief that this movie is a must see for black males to move past gay bashing, homophobic jokes/ quips, and to restore what true masculinity is and should be. Masculinity and the growing up of a black male should be based in the maturity to stand firm in who you are and not the fear of what others will perceive you to be while protecting the rights of all around us to do the exact same in their journey through this world.

To my gay friends, frat bothers, neighbors, sport stars, poets and all those who hide in plain sight out of fear: I truly hope the day comes when movies like this are no longer needed to cause reflection of these biases we hold as a Nation. Until then grab a friend, be uncomfortable if you must, and come out more male then when you went in not because you are transformed but because you are willing to transcend the limitations of what this society wants us to be: animals with no soul. We are strong. We are black and we need each other in this fight called life. Forgive my ignorance if I ever treated you less than the men that you are.

Sincerely,
Your brother

AFTER THE RAIN FALLS

Phobias

Phobias are types of anxiety disorders that causes a person
to experience extreme fear.
Arachnophobia the fear of spiders.
Hydrophobia the fear of water-
think of the difficulty in bathing, baptism or healing from
Claustrophobia
the feeling of being trapped in closed spaces.
Interesting-How these enclosed stages have become places
for me to face my fears.

So you can imagine, how I felt in the baseball locker room
When the picture of my friend kissing a man, fell out of his pocket.
His tears-gathering in the corners of his eyes.
He sat.
I stared.
Feeling ashamed,
as I realized that my friend was waiting for me
to cast punishment on him for simply existing.

Then I remembered how just last week,
Boys tied a boy to a field goal post,
stripped him naked while
painting faggot into his reddening skin with fists.

Remembered how just last month a black boy was strung to
a pick-up truck by his ankles,

rope digging into his bones and drug two miles until his skin burned off
until the white resembled, them.

Remembered how last year a boy who was both-Black and gay placed a gun to his temple,
pulled the trigger,
decided that he would rather make love to a bullet in death
Than be bullied in a world where he can't love.

Remembered how community made excuses for boys just having fun,
How courts showed phobias of issuing jail sentences for hate crimes.

Sitting in the locker room, We could hear our teammates footsteps coming echoing the hate of the 60's.

In good ole Alabama, we play baseball,
We shout ROLL TIDE!
And yes, We know that it is dangerous for men to be black
But it is even more dangerous to also be gay.

The marginalized and oppressed have become phobias.
Black or gay, are things to be feared.
Chalk lines and yellow caution tape
Drape both equally as if we are living etch a sketches
to be used and tossed out when done.

Black and gay bodies become beautifully broken concrete graffiti

AFTER THE RAIN FALLS

to lay as reminders to neither be Black nor gay
less you be hunted.

While the picture lay on the ground,
I questioned, why do phobics run from or attack things?
For me, I wanted to run because the picture staring back at
me was a reminder of my ugly.
His eyes gazing at another man-my insecurity
that a woman would never love me with that same passion
or honesty.

In high school, I knew that he was black.
Did not know that he was gay.
Knew he was man each time he helped fix the knot in my tie,
change my tire by the expressway,
or fixed my palms to shoot a pistol properly
Just in case the good ole boys came in sheets at night.

Even though my father raised me Christian.
Gay was frowned at in my house.
I learned well from community
to not love gay,
How to hate what was different.

I picked up the picture
wrinkled with my homophobia.
Hid the picture in my pocket
before our teammates came in.

When they were gone
And the locker room was safe,

TIMOTHY "URBAN THOUGHTS" MOORE

I returned his picture with a handshake.

We walked silently.
Me into my home.
Him into his home.

I wonder if that's what they meant by homophobia?
His house next to mine,
A secret in between.

Tears For My Daughter

My daughter, Asha, looked up at me and asked me daddy,
Daddy, why are you crying?
I told her these tears are not for you
But of you.
These tears are of the same fabric that weave time
Around love clichés, DNA, and poet's ink blots.

These tears are of the very moment that checking under your bed
And patting your head while reading bed time stories will one day fade.
The moment that one day I will no longer create invisible castles
for princesses to dwell safely on a ribbon in the sky in Nashville during Christmas.

We spend moments sharing tears-me and her delaying her departure
And each tear a little less of my soul to give this Earth.
It breaks from the understanding of love being suffering sometimes
Giving back nutrients of me to this Earth to keep her- here, with me.

I hold her unflinching of her desire to never admit injury.
She is part dare devil always exploring.
These tears are the portals to the future

TIMOTHY "URBAN THOUGHTS" MOORE

That I dare monsters to step through
And those damn monsters are coming.

Coming to damage your heart,
to tear you apart
and make this distance be our Dragon.

These tears are for the moments
that the monster in your closet is no longer shadows of a coat tail,
But cute light skin men with good hair,
who sing and will pretend to love you just to get tail.

Of every single Facebook, Skype, Facetime, Twitter Hashtag -I miss you.
I use social media to close the distance from Memphis to Nashville.
Not to blame anyone but when young produce young you get disconnects
That you spend your adult years trying to fix
One sided stories, change perspective when the truth is between Memphis
And Nashville, watching your mom leave with you
Before I could even draw your face fully in my mind,
212 miles and 30 steps to your front door.
I cry for three hours on the drive back from you.
These are the tears of frustration of every man who cares enough to cry for daughters.
These tears are of that exact moment that I prepare you mentally for the first date that will come.
I refuse to wait too late to let your idea of a good man
be left to images of television
or fate.

AFTER THE RAIN FALLS

I will not wait to open the car door
or help you should you fall to the floor.
I will not sit and linger on societal premises that chivalry is dead.
Oh yes, these tears are of the moments that I refused to call you, Barbie
because my last name is not Mattel but Moore
and your first name is not BOSS but Asha
named after old Okinawan for 'new life.'
You have no choice but to always be new
and strong and effortlessly you.

Baby girl, these tears are not for you but of you,
of all the moments that I will forgive you,
and love you,
and pray for you.
These tears are of each moment that I see your reflection
in every mirror that I pass.
Of each morning for 17 years that I have awoke without you under another roof
And I cried that single tear hoping that one day you can forgive
Me for not letting you see me cry enough.
You are my heart and if you ever doubt it for a second...
Know this, that your father is so proud
And will always cry for you.

Three Letters

(For Bon-Ton, my Uncle, and Edward)

I.

I never saw three letters that could paralyze a man worse than having to say I love you
Until I saw my friend get diagnosed with three single letters that strike fear in the hearts
of even your worse adversary
Causing dads to cry for their sons, H-I-V

We thought we had heard him wrong when he said it to the class
It was then that I first saw a man's soul break
I never saw a man truly cry
Until I saw my classmate fall
And the others refuse to pick him up
For fear of it rubbing off on them

I remember watching his knees turn callused with bruises over the coming months
Each day bringing him further and further from smiling
I remember hearing him pray
And knowing deep down that GOD had to have heard him so when he died
I was shocked.

AFTER THE RAIN FALLS

I remember his mama sprawled cursing GOD bitter
His dad head down buried in shame
And words thrown around like GAY
Like being Gay somehow made his life less valuable
Guess it was just easier attaching HIV to gay
So that others would feel safe

TIMOTHY "URBAN THOUGHTS" MOORE

II.

I remember my father pausing after drinks got switched
two Pepsi's
two straws
he paused
my uncle offering to just buy another
I remember my father just telling my uncle it was okay
and sipped slowly
I didn't understand

Until the car came up missing that summer
Police said they found it sold for two hundred from an addict
That grew bold with each hit
Dividing family into victims
Supporters and enablers
Hijackers of affection
At his funeral
The words recovered drug addict were used
Like his vice was bigger or that much more evil
than those who hustle lies
and cheat for a living

AFTER THE RAIN FALLS

III.

I remember the story first heard over lunch
A co-worker's brother whom I never met
But from the stories seemed familiar
To have an artistic spirit
Love martial arts
And died young reminded me of me
While I listened intently trying to find new ways to avoid an outcome

At his repast the echoes of youth were heard
Mourning along the halls of that place where death lay
And what does it matter
To the remaining who still live dangerously
Who still ignore those three letters

TIMOTHY "URBAN THOUGHTS" MOORE

Scars

After death came knocking with full intention to take me,
after bullets broke flesh and grazed me,
after the stab wounds,
knife wounds,
broken bones,
shattered lungs,
collapsed veins,
flipped cars,
pain killer addiction,
the grief,
survivor remorse,
a cord around my neck at birth,
frozen hypothermic body,
mental depressive breaks,
and suicide attempt after suicide attempt...
...I died.
pulse going beep,
stop. pause. continue.
pulse going beep. stop. stop. beep. continue twice,
named dead I was brought back,
glass imprinted into my face,
cars crashing into my place,
doors busted,
fight, after fight,
after fight, after fight,

AFTER THE RAIN FALLS

against fibromyalgia,
leukemia,
I stand, laughing.
God still is.
I am still; here.
#Onward

TIMOTHY "URBAN THOUGHTS" MOORE

A Love Letter To America

Dear America,
I wanted to write you a love letter.
Each line starts with the best of intentions
But I get lost when you pass me by on Twitter/X spaces
Or keep hiring quarterbacks that are half of Kaepernick's talent.

And I noticed on Facebook your status has changed to single.
Instagram only shows pictures of what I did for you:
The inventions, ideas, and the beautiful cotton dress that I handpicked for you
But I guess there is an error.
My blackness is cropped out of all the images of me standing next to you in history books.
Rumor is-in some cities it's illegal to teach about how I loved you.

Baby, I got questions about your love for me.
I mean it's supposed to be Just us?
Wouldn't that be justice
Us cuddled comparing memories of our crazy exes
Jim Crow and the Queen?
But you seem to have forgotten because you keep treating me like a side piece.
I'm confused as to how you can do that like I Ain't A Man.

You only bring me to the kitchen to cook
But never to sit at the table where your family is eating.

AFTER THE RAIN FALLS

The candlelight dinner shows my skin tone.
You think it's beautiful but only when I'm being athletic.
And you, you ignore me, when I talk about police brutality.
As if I too, can't sing America.

America, stop lying about loving me.
It would be okay if your last name was Disney
You'd be my Queen and I, your King.
And you wouldn't be leaving this Scar of tattooed hashtags
followed by the blackboy names that you keep leaving in your wake-

Dismissed Valentine's
Because you didn't like the tea
or the skittles,
CD's,
Or the way I tried to just breathe while hugging you back

This relationship resembles the fragileness of chalk lines
That mark the bodies of the beautiful black men you used to love
America, is your last name Kardashian?
The way you love me and then find me later not doing so good?
Just broken and tired in a shell of who I used to be before you loved me

I'm tired of being used to elevate your celebrity.
You say you love me,
But where's justice between just us?
The sad part I'm still in love with you, America.
Even if you won't give me the liberty
of loving me back.

TIMOTHY "URBAN THOUGHTS" MOORE

Truthfully,
I know that you are toxic.
I just can't help but see the potential of what you could be.

Oh, say can you see?

AFTER THE RAIN FALLS

Smiles

Black boys be buried

before being born. Brought

back broken, bodies bombarded

by beatings: Black boys

can't be smiling 'til

caskets drop and the

mortician fixes our smiles.

TIMOTHY "URBAN THOUGHTS" MOORE

Enter

Enter represents the most important key on the keyboard for a writer.
It represents the completion of an idea of a space or project.

Black boy enters.
Black boy enters room.
Black boy smile enters first.
People wave as he enters.
Black boy sits at his computer.
Writes first line and presses enter after each carefully crafted line.

He writes about how cool it is to pay big mamas bills with first job as writer: Enter.
About how black boys invent cool stuff and create cool jobs: Enter.
About how beautifully brilliant black boys in the Bronx became chess champions: Enter.
Black boy smiles,
Black boy gives papers to editor.
Editor types back:
"Not good enough- put some more realness in it-you, know that good hood stuff."

Black boy presses delete on history.
Black boy presses keys until they spoke of current topics of black liberation of thought,

AFTER THE RAIN FALLS

Of Physics,
of Wakanda,
and how blacks in comic books are the first to be deleted,
Before they even hit the stage, story or big screen how our stories have to fight
and escape just to be seen on white paper.
Black boy presses enter and the editor replies, "No, son It's not enough death in it. Put some more death in it."

Black boy gets angry: presses Ctrl + Alt + Delete: must be an error.
Black recording keeps looping truth. Must be an error.
He tries to write about white-on-white violence but the paper wouldn't take it.
He Talks about how two blacks, both poor fought for some money and a name over a girl
But guess it's only romantic- if Shakespeare framed it: Enter. Editor rejected that too.
Editor said, "Press enter for the last time, boy. Do you want this job, boy?"

Black boy writes of other black boys shooting
fadeaways on courts taking the last shot- Enter
Of how a black girl came up missing – correction-
Press option -remove black with white - Enter
Because everyone knows Rikeshia's don't get any alerts
Black boy of how a gang broke into a store and stole food-
Leave out that they were hungry.
That will make villains have too much humanity and ruin storylines.
Black boy presses Enter.

TIMOTHY "URBAN THOUGHTS" MOORE

Editor says, "Good job! notates a smiley face emoji
Presses Enter in response with a note to check account for funds."

Black boy leaves work and enters the Space bar.
The bartender asks, "What would you like to drink?"
The black boy says, "Something strong like patience,
Like overcoming,
Like writing what you want when you want,
Like I quit today,
Like I ain't got no bills to worry 'bout,

Like Black folks tired of writing other people stories,
Like Black people trauma shouldn't just be good for poetry points,
Like stop using our agony for your profit,
Like big mama gone be good off these words one day,
Like big mama gone be good off our words one day,
Like a long island with a shift of alcohol!"
The bartender asks, "What happened today- brother?"
I reply, "Nothing much, I just learned how to stomach entering corporate America
While pressing,

Enter."

AFTER THE RAIN FALLS

Spades

In the game of spades, the Spade becomes the most powerful family in the deck.
Having the ability to alter course,
overcome all,
and to win challenges
The Queen of Spades is one of the most powerful cards in the deck
which makes me wonder:
Did Kate ever play Spades?

Did she ever see how powerful she was?
If she ever just held herself in her hands,
looked down in the mirror and saw that she too was a spade.
Built powerful,
Strong,
Wanted
And beautiful.
I wonder if she knew that she was loved more than her bags or the baggage inside them that we all carry.
Males and females lugging carefully crafted carriers around.

We all playing the game-packing our emotions
in empty vessels that we paint cute,
acceptable
hiding the contents of our spirits.
Toting the darkness along for hidden journeys
latching and zipping away family secrets and burdens

that only we will know.
Hanging it carefully on handles,
doors,
desks
and tables.

Inside our homes and on our persons to hide our wealth of insecurities.
We carry careful not to scratch the outside
for the fear of the depression spilling out.
We are good at keeping our bags-
our compartment contents
From being discovered,
after all they increase value after the artist is gone away.
After the holder of the bags of ugly are gone,
The contents: character traits, DNA coded to self-destruct,
mental illnesses that lay next to the prescriptions
and flight bottles of vodka that save cost at bars.

We spike drinks to drown sorrow quicker
and after we drink too much and we fall.
Bags crashing to earth.
People staring at the contents with questions.
What is all this?
She seemed so well?
So put together?
So perfect?
So rich?
Her family pictures will show everything but her burdens,
Her worries,
Her fears.

AFTER THE RAIN FALLS

But the bags, the bags will be declared works of art
and found beautiful.
The creator- damaged, flawed.
Labeled could have done better
as if she never wanted to create herself into the perfect bag-
capable of carrying all the crap safely.

I wonder if Kate Spade ever saw her Spades
as being worthy of being more than just bags
I wonder if Kate Spade ever saw herself
as being more than just bags.
Or if she was like me, always just trying
to find the right one manly enough to put all my stuff in.

I wonder if Kate Spade ever knew how many loved her
more than her bags?

TIMOTHY "URBAN THOUGHTS" MOORE

Stained Glass

(dedicated to Tywanza Sanders age 26 who lost his life trying to save his aunt Susie Jackson age 87)

Greetings good church folks, Welcome to Emanuel AME church in Charleston, South Carolina.
My name is Tywanza Sanders.
I just wanted to welcome you to the home,
where I pray.
I wanted to show you my church.
What's that you say?
Oh yes. Yes. I do apologize.
I forgot to mention that my church got redecorated the other Sunday.
We got new stained windows that day.
Don't worry. We are okay.
We prayed continuously so that paint job
just blessings covering destruction.
Over there are some splatter paint pictures of my future casts on walls.
As if my Blackness, was not enough to paint
The designer decided on some red to add a splash of color.

Guess, this church needed a deeper hue of my spirit
so Jesus wept while the coloring of these walls occurred.
Color of a sinners choosing.
But I, I won't linger there or on the fact that all these prayers held intact.
Held me here to attempt to be Superman.

AFTER THE RAIN FALLS

I deflected as many bullets as I could,
as my body would, but truth is I am not Superman.
I am just a man who came to pray today.
Not to sacrifice on the altar.
I came to give prayers not to become a prayer.

Many will seek revenge, writing of my sorrow on social media
to avenge the hailstorms from hell he brought.
Truth is that I represent every murder untold
and hid in shadows
and corners of America.
This ain't the first Church to be redecorated without invitation.

In South Carolina, where the roads of slavery are marked
with the names of our ancestor's owners,
We drive. On concrete etched with the arrogance
to keep themselves wealthy,
Forgive them, for they know exactly what they do.

This bloodletting of America. It ain't new.
This is just the newest revision of the King James Bible
written transcribed by mortals who never wanted the full story to be told.
I grow bold. Here at my church,
at the heart of the African-American church.
We survived. Bombs. Arson. Shotgun blasts.
Moltov Cocktail explosions and spray-painted bigotry.
We are still here and yes, I died.
But oh, how I died here at home
so that you could come to church.

TIMOTHY "URBAN THOUGHTS" MOORE

Bury me with the same blood-stained pews I laid against.
Use that good wood for my casket.
Folks gone think it's custom.
People will think it's an expensive crimson casket
and call it beautiful.

Call me beautiful and I am.
It has always been beautiful
to come back home.

AFTER THE RAIN FALLS

Cry

Babies first official cry is a beautiful sight to behold.
It shows the doctors and the world that the babies' lungs are working.
It is a good thing.
Babies that are silent are made to cry.

Whether girl or boy, they cry.
I watched my sister fall once and my mom and dad picked her up.
Dusted her off.
Let her cry.
Let her explain her pain.
Let her process the falling.
Let her hurt.
Allowed her space to grieve herself.
She eventually felt better and was given a pink band-aid.
She learned that crying is okay.

I saw a boy fall on the same playground.
His family.
Told him to shush all that.
Told him get up.
Told him dust himself off.
Told him be a man.
Man up.
That men don't...
That girls cry.

TIMOTHY "URBAN THOUGHTS" MOORE

When I was young, I saw my classmate Frank get sucker punched
By a guy twice his size.
His dad told him to man up.
Wipe the blood, the dirt, ball up your fist and strike.
He ain't supposed to...
Told that men don't ...
Like girls, cause girls can cry.
Boys, Boys can just...

My best friend Willie Brown, Jr. hung himself in Tuskegee.
His suicide note didn't have any tear marks.
When I found out, I was told to go to school.
Got to school, teachers said Black boys die.
Said, "Get over it."
Said, "Pray bout it."
Said, "Time heals."
I stared at the clock.
I'm 42 and I'm still staring.
Wondering if all the second marks were the remnants of tears.
I remember being told a lot of things to do that day
but never that it was okay for a man, to...

Saw my friend get shot and die in front of me.
At his funeral, a dozen men held tear drops like grenades.
Afraid to drop them for the fear of harming the others.
Lynch pins in hands.
Shades holding the solemn in,
We all staring at each other,
dry faced you know–
Being men.

AFTER THE RAIN FALLS

Cause men don't ...
We can't...

We've learned to mask our emotions and limit ourselves to anger or joy.
Get straight faced is the motto.
I remember watching my father bury his once.
I saw his father close the casket on his often.
It was adulthood before I learned how to...
Cause men don't...
Men be tough.
Men be bold.
Men be tanks rolling over and destroying boys imploding them
With the trauma of war that we never learned how to unpack.
Cause girls cry but boys...
Boys just hurt.
Boys just rage.
Boys bet not shed no tear.
Bet not.
But what if we do?

Does it prove us different
Or human
That we are capable of sorrow?
Or seeing something so beautiful that it moves us.
I saw a ballet once and the music made my heart swell.
I saw my daughter Asha dance for the first time and I felt it.
I cried and it was beautiful.
I'm not ashamed of that
But I am ashamed that the distance between us now is hard for me to process.

TIMOTHY "URBAN THOUGHTS" MOORE

All the days, I taught and loved kids
While you were dancing.
All the conversations of a parent convinced to make a father other than.
But I couldn't the one time I did
Was spun in court as an unstable man.
Now all the proof is there but years of lies taint truths
That making sure you prospered had a cost.
All these stages, all this work, all this community...
It all has a cost
But it never meant for a second
Meant That I wasn't crying over you each night while praying.
That sometimes that when I should,
Maybe I could,
I'll find the words one day to in conversation to explain it all.
Show you all the letters and gifts I sent.
All the photos of you, I still hold.
Until then I am trying to remember if my lungs work.

Doctor can I?
God can?
Daughter?
Can you remind me how to cry?
I promise, I'll be man enough to
This time.

AFTER THE RAIN FALLS

For My Grandpa
(Dedicated to Harrel C. Moore, Sr.)

When the leaves find the ground
In fall
They find the colors fading from green to brown
To gold

Floating back to Earth
As they whisper prayers
Gravity takes hold
The tree lets go

Fall starts
This is nature's jazz
Treble and bass notes
Balancing the metronome of the seasons

As they must
For each of us
Family members and friends have become melodies
Crashing into each other waiting

On Grandpa to tell us about
Dizzy or Charlie or Jelly Roll
We waited.
Tucking prayer cards in pews and bibles and hearts

TIMOTHY "URBAN THOUGHTS" MOORE

My God!
We waited on the chorus to form the extemporaneous moment
That deciphers jazz from just a regular song
This song was so special.

We wanted it to last forever
Our rest notes taking breath in the pauses of respirators
Between sheets that became hugs
We were all falling,

Moving up and down
Wailing out loud
The joy and sorrow of such a beautiful solo that we watched
The breathing of his chest

The courage of years of learning how jazz works
How unapologetic Blackness works
How being a man works
The irony not lost that we don't decide when the melody ends

Just the start of the count of when the beat starts
And what we do with the progress of the music within
The final curtain call came in the night
Memories flooded in morning

Our tears falling
The best solos that we can create in between the measures
Our arms became music sheets
Our palms psalms uplifted to the sky

AFTER THE RAIN FALLS

God collected a beautiful song that day
I remember witnessing clouds drift by
I watched them angry that I didn't hear the song anymore
Until the wind blew

And I caught it
The melody
The rift
The softness of the moment

That exists in the knowing that
All along we were praying for an awakening
And we were the ones in the coma
Cause he was teaching us that the awakening

Is in the knowing of the living
And my God
Did he live and do it his way
As if his last name was Sinatra

And not Moore
Let the sun come
Let Heaven become a part of our hearts
Become a part of the song

Awaken the music
Of family and children's joys
This is a legacy song
Connecting the African diaspora to the field hollers to the blues to the jazz

TIMOTHY "URBAN THOUGHTS" MOORE

Is committed to our memory
We hear the consistency coursing through our blood streams
On all the winds for all to hear
We sat on the edges of beds.
Watching the leaf golden and ripened with age
Tumble through the sky like the sweetest saxophones solo
Or the greatest drummers staccato
Or the most complete piano chords

The silence in the song was as equally as beautiful
As the loud
It has taught me the beauty of the song
This is the beauty of jazz

That at any given moment,
The song can find a new way to begin
Again
When the leaves find the ground in fall

They find the colors fading from green to brown
To gold
floating back to Earth as they whisper prayers
Gravity takes hold

the tree lets go
Fall starts
This is nature's jazz
This is the music.

Wrong Woman

I like you.
I can love you;
BUT,
I can't battle your trauma.
I can't exorcise your demons.
That work
Is for GOD and a therapist to heal you.

All I can do is support:
Offer prayer,
Lead meditation,
Pick up your pills,
And a bill-
Or Three
To help you with your co-pays,
While letting you go.

TIMOTHY "URBAN THOUGHTS" MOORE

When They Tell You That You Are Dying—

Empty fills the room.
Doctor stares at me.
Nurse says, "I am so sorry."
This is the third opinion.
Do you have a question?
Naw. Not really, I mean to say:

6 months is nothing but a bunch of days.
A small number of sunsets left.
How you pronounce Leukemia?
Is denial and acceptance the same thing?
My hair fell out.
Looked like a black river flowing to the drain.

I remember when the first clump fell out at the dinner table.
My sister squeezed my hand like she was putting prayers back.
I remember telling my parents.
I remember the silence.
It was the loudest thing I've ever heard.
I remember telling my fraternity line brothers and their faces.

How do you break the news and be your own anchor?
How you say- dying?
How do you pronounce your life to be quiet?

AFTER THE RAIN FALLS

Ain't it ironic for a poet to leave the page empty?
Remember me not slamming anymore?
Perfect scores seemed less important than trying to keep score of the days left,

Or crinkled corners on ya three daughter's faces,
Or the teardrops your friends kept catching.
I remember the bed and how my fingers curled to the sheets.
I remember how my vomit became my morning ritual to a porcelain god
That never granted the prayer for it all to stop.
Remember how my spirit was at ease with the sleeping.

I fell in a great relationship with death.
She was unrelenting.
I buried my aunt; her breast covered in pink ribbons.
My family member- his prostate a problem that we never could figure out.
And WE still are solving for all the Black women, we loved.
I remember how the radiation withered my tattoos.

But I had a praying grandmother- Who would move mountains,
Who jumped up and shouted, "...but you still breathing!"
Yelled, "You ain't dead yet;
You got's work to do!"
A church and a Pastor Earle who said, "Man know not the hour."
Had a praise in my heart that said chemo is just a process.

Radical faith that knew this radiation is just my body editing.
I got more poems to write.

TIMOTHY "URBAN THOUGHTS" MOORE

My throat became a war ground for battle cries in between treatments.
Doctors said, "We don't understand."
Nurses said, "Gotta be the wrong chart."
Medical staff waiting on me to say something.

I said, "I feel different."
My body carrying pounds from steroids and stress but my steps are light.
And maybe this ain't a poem anymore- but a sermon.
A broken hallelujah.
A shout from the motherboard.
A proclamation that- I'm still; here.

The doctors can't explain where it all went away to.
But I can,
In a poem that ends like this...
BUT GOD;
And let the church say:
Amen.

AFTER THE RAIN FALLS

To My Father
(Harrel, Jr.)

I lamented how to end this poetry book. Should I close with a poem, an essay, a haiku, a short thought or another conversation? In the end, I will close with the only thing that makes sense. I will write my father a love letter.

Dear Dad,
For everyone that knows us, God bless they have seen our ups and downs. You have been a good father and a better man. Now that I have three girls of my own: Iyanla, Asha, and Imani- I see clearly now the pressures that come with the title of dad. Being a father is a daunting task. Every single day, I wake up and try to figure out life, bills, how to love them so that they grow strong. I try to be a good man to my woman.
I have failed.
I have succeeded.
I have maintained.
I have and am love to them as best as I can be.
At times, I have just tried to figure it out.
Others I've done pretty well.

Balancing long distance with my first daughter Asha with being young made me learn the hard way that the small moments count. I'm still trying to find the love you had for me for when I turned my back on you for all those years. You never let me forget that you loved me. Trying to adopt and care for Iyanla made me realize that patience is a virtue in confidence building. Your innate ability to guide me through all my creativity to hone into my purpose is truly amazing. Losing Emmanuel to a miscarriage taught me what it takes to hold a family together. You've held ours together and mom for my entire life and before that. Gaining Imani taught me to forgive. I've learned that it all has a purpose. It all has a moment in our life to teach us the lessons that we must learn or we repeat the pattern. You told me this when I was 15. I was caught up in the glitter of money and the streets. I had to come to a place where time could be my teacher.

Being a creative and thinker, my life has taken many paths. Some great and others terrible but they were mine to own. I find myself now at 42 looking at my girls and my family and understanding that sacrifices must be made to endure. You sacrificed so much looking back and you never complained. Seeing you smile is joy in itself. Your hugs make everything okay. I know that one day life physically will part us but this is my eternal love language. These words were often all I had when I found myself in dark circumstances.

This writing has held me when I have lost my way. In the darkness, the streets, homelessness, joblessness, transition, sickness, and depression episodes- this poetry has held me. I pray that this open letter closes this chapter and brings us into a new one full of adventure and joy. Whatever the chapter is to hold, I know we will be beside each other as best friends. You are my best friend. I respect you and honor you pops.

Ironic, when people say how good a father I am-I still wonder what they see. I am trying so hard. I still don't have it all figured out. I say thank you then quickly tell them you should meet my dad. It is true. You are a better father than me. I am getting there. Each day seems more urgent to get it right. The facts are you raised five kids who are all amazing people. We all graduated college, 3 hold Master's degrees, one holds a Doctorate degree and yeah me- your knucklehead of the crew went on to a Master's degree from The University of Memphis and spending a cohort at Massachusetts Institute of Technology (MIT), receiving a Congressional Certificate for Education and community service from the United States of America Congress signed by the President along with over 30 other awards for education and poetry. I look back and realize what you were teaching me.

It is not the failures or successes of a man, it is simply how he carries himself in between.

This book is dedicated to many and I know some of the ideas are too liberal for us to agree on but God bless your heart for understanding that the fire that is inside me had to receive oxygen and space to flourish. The one takeaway is I hope that everyone that encounters this book sees that Black men are so much more than anger. We are not monolithic beings. We have so many emotions and such complex ideals of breath and love.

With all that I close this book and this chapter of my writing journey with a simple thought. I just want to say that I love you, Dad. I publicly acknowledge you as the greatest man that I know. Without you I never would have matured and without my mom I never would have embraced being the poet that I am. I am forever grateful of parents that never gave up on me even when at times I literally and physically gave up on myself at times. You both saw the best in me and that is the blessing of parenthood that I am learning.

With my whole heart and love,
Your son
Timothy L. Moore (Urban Thoughts)

Epilogue

Black male self-care is a radical act. Part of this self-care includes having the ability (time, space, and resources) to express ourselves in ways that fuel our soul. Timothy "Urban Thoughts" Moore has done this in *After the Rain Falls*. From "Struggle" to "Smiles" to "Birthday Candles," Moore pulls back the curtain to showcase Black men's deepest thoughts, worries, and pains.

As a sociologist, I found "Invisible Hoodies" and "Black Diamonds" particularly insightful. "Invisible Hoodies" contextualizes how being a Black man in America operates as a hoodie that supposedly criminalizes us. Moore's words amplify research on policing and criminalization, and symbolically highlights the killing of Trayvon Martin. Martin was a 17-year-old killed by George Zimmerman in Sanford, Florida in 2012. Martin was leaving a convenience store with a bottle of iced tea and a bag of skittles, simply aiming to return home to watch the second half of the NBA all-star game. However, he was followed and surveilled by Zimmerman (the self-appointed neighborhood watchman), leading to a violent encounter that left Martin shot dead by Zimmerman. The incident started the Black Lives Matter movement. Moore eloquently illuminates how some political pundits aimed to blame Martin's death on the hoodie he was wearing rather than Black male criminalization, stereotyping, and racism.

For many African Americans, Martin's death embodied how "Black males are often killed with impunity," as I have written in academic articles with Dr. Keon Gilbert. On one hand, police violence impacts Black males more than other groups. Black teenagers like Martin are 21 times more likely than White teenagers to be killed by police. Tamir Rice in Cleveland, Ohio comes to mind; however, Rice was 12-years-old and had not quite reached the 13-year-old pinnacle to claim teenagerhood. Similar to George Floyd, Rice does represent the most troubling statistic of all, which is the fact that Blacks are 3.5 times more likely than Whites to be killed by police when they are unarmed and not attacking. Rice was with his sister in a park playing with a toy gun, like many kids do. Police shot and killed him in less than three seconds. The context described above is the profoundness of "Invisible Hoodies." It illuminates how every day, mundane acts of being human lead to different outcomes for Black males and contributes to these troubling statistics.

But, if a person is reading too fast, they may miss the significance of one of the stats above. While a Black person is killed every 40 hours by law enforcement in the United States, Black people are significantly killed more than White people when they are unarmed and not attacking. This suggest that there is something greater than an actual threat driving these outcomes. Well, my research documents that anti-Blackness and racism drive these statistics. The "Invisible Hoodie" represents that Black male bodies are perceived as dangerous and needing to be tamed even when we are not doing anything but breathing air.

Black men understand this. Moore understands this, as he chronicles the "#BlackBoyRules." The implementation of these rules is what sociologists call a "signaling process." This signaling process aims to convey a sensibility to unarm others of a perceived threat and implement "politics of respectability," even if we know some of these strategies may have a limited impact. Black men think more consciously about their clothing, where they exercise, and how they need to express a "softer" presentation of self in predominately White spaces to get out unscathed.

Altogether, anti-Blackness often drives racial disparities in police killings. And, while Black communities are overpoliced, they are also underserved. A person living in a predominately Black community is less likely to have access to healthcare resources and have first responders arrive during a medical emergency.

Even if Black men survive their "Invisible Hoodies," thriving is often elusive. Research I have conducted with colleagues shows that Black men's mental health suffers in neighborhoods that are plagued with more police violence. Consequently, Black men have higher rates of depression and anxiety. And, yet, they are less likely to utilize healthcare to get treated when they do have access. In this regard, they may worry about medical mistreatment and a lack of cultural competency of healthcare providers.

So, Black men's physical health is ransacked. Their mental health is then negatively impacted by these physical health ramifications. And, we have not even gotten to emotional health, self-care, and Black men's ability to express themselves. This is why self-care and self-expression are radical acts. This is why Moore's book about what to do "After the Rain Falls" is so poetic. Moore encourages us to express ourselves to become "Black Diamonds" like "stars in the sky" who are "loved." I think love is an authentic and basic goal. Loved by whom? Well, I think by everyone. Loved so that when someone sees a Black boy walking down the street that they are not in fear of "Invisible Hoodies" or feel the need to surveil and police them. Rather, they feel the need to express equitable love.
-Dr. Rashawn Ray

Dr. Rashawn Ray is a Professor of Sociology and leads the University of Maryland's Social Justice Alliance in collaboration with Bowie State University as well as the Anti-Black Racism Initiative housed in the College of Behavioral and Social Sciences. He is also a Senior Fellow at The Brookings Institution. Ray's research addresses the mechanisms that manufacture and maintain racial and social inequity (biography via the University of Maryland directory). He is a widely acknowledged as one of the brightest minds in his field. Dr. Ray is influential at developing high level ideas and researching at a critical level - the next steps to a better world.

Acknowledgements

Thank-you to God for providing me with such a gift. My ancestors, family, friends and all my supporters (Thinkers) and all those who have gone before me: I love you.

Thank-you to Alpha Phi Alpha Fraternity, Inc., for surrounding me with men who always wanted to transcend.

I acknowledge the contributions of Dr. Rashawn Ray, Dr. Ernest Gibson III, Speak Life Society, Shandy Riddle, Tundrea Lyons-Brock, Deanna Chavers, Amber Carter with ANC Proofreading Services, Indiana Tuggle with Victory Publishing / IndiWrites, Free Fyre, The Watering Hole (I see you tribe!), my forever muse Andrea Fincher, Dasan Ahanu, Memphis Art and Poetry Community, Memphis Sponsors and Funders of my art, all of my students (you have taught me at times), Asia Samson, Natalie Richardson-Johnson, Angelo Geter, Christella Francois, Michelle Dodd, Jay Ward, Christopher "Truth B. Told" Owens, the late Ullysses Jones, Jr., the late Ullysses Jones, III., Mama Jones, the late Willie Brown, Jr., my family, the writings of Langston Hughes, the writings of James Baldwin, and the writings of Nikki Giovanni.

TIMOTHY "URBAN THOUGHTS" MOORE

I acknowledge you and thank-you because you didn't have to love a boy from Tuskegee, AL (Roll Tide!) who became a man in Memphis, TN (901 Mane). May the blessings bestowed upon me from my village find their way back to you ten-fold.

Sincerely,
Timothy "Urban Thoughts" Moore
#Onward

www.ingramcontent.com/pod-product-compliance
Lightning Source LLC
Chambersburg PA
CBHW061748070526
44585CB00025B/2831